Servant Hearts

The Legacy of the Dimmitt Automotive Group

By

Richard R. Dimmitt

With

Tom McQueen

Copyright © 2012
by Richard R. Dimmitt with Tom McQueen

Servant Hearts
The Legacy of the Dimmitt Automotive Group
by Richard R. Dimmitt with Tom McQueen

Printed in the United States of America

ISBN 9781624191930

All rights reserved solely by the author. The author guarantees all contents are original and do not infringe upon the legal rights of any other person or work. No part of this book may be reproduced in any form without the permission of the author. The views expressed in this book are not necessarily those of the publisher.

www.xulonpress.com

Table of Contents

1. Book Praise vii
2. Dedication ix
3. Foreword xi
4. Introduction xiii
5. Embracing the Brand 21
6. Our Mission 29
7. Our Values 33
8. Our Pledge 46
9. Developing the Right Leaders 51
10. Hiring the Right People 59
11. The Language of Loyalty 63
12. Guest Service Standards 71
13. Respect 75
14. Trust 79
15. Being Genuine 83
16. Compassion 87
17. Change 90
18. Dimmitt Center for Learning 93
19. Service in America Today 98
20. The Six Roadblocks to Legendary Service 105
21. Overcoming Negativism 112
22. Curing Corporate Cancer 118
23. Coaching Is Key 126

24. Emotional Intelligence and Coaching 135
25. A Coaching Process That Works 154
26. Making It Fun 165
27. Sustainable Competitive Advantage 169
28. The Three Gifts of a Servant's Heart 173
29. What Does the Future Hold? 181
30. Personal Invitation 185
31. Biographies 187

Book Praise

"*Servant Hearts* is a powerful and practical roadmap for achieving a sustainable competitive advantage in today's marketplace. Make this required reading for the leaders in your organization."
        Matthew Kelly
        New York Times Best-Selling Author of
        The Dream Manager

"As a loyal guest who has enjoyed the Dimmitt experience, I'm proud to recommend *Servant Hearts* as a resource for improving your business."
        Brittany Lincicome
        LPGA Champion

"The wisdom contained in *Servant Hearts* will revitalize and energize any business. If you live out the principles in this book, you will create an enterprise with a positive corporate culture that will prosper in any market condition."
        Mark Tallman, President
        MBTI Group

"*Servant Hearts* is a book that will enlighten organizations that truly want to understand the importance of customer service in today's ever-changing marketplace. I highly recommend it to leaders who strive to build a service-based culture as a driver of long-term business success."
>David Archibald, President
>Rolls-Royce Motor Cars NA LLC

Dedication

To Richard and Peter and the entire
community at Dimmitt…
May you continue to grow in Faith, Love, and Hope
as you commit yourself to serve one another, our
guests, and those in need in the Tampa Bay region.

Foreword

*I*f you believe that running a business is easy in today's marketplace, then you need to think again.

For the first time in history, we're faced with understanding the wants, needs, and desires of four generations of buyers. In addition, short attention spans, time demands, and new technologies all factor into a commercial sphere that is both intense and vigorously competitive.

Richard Dimmitt, his wife Doreen, and their sons, Rick and Peter, understand all of this. For nearly one hundred years, their family has firmly held on to a belief that eludes many companies today. They know that achieving a sustainable competitive advantage in the twenty-first century requires that a business be infused with the spirit of a servant's heart.

No matter the generation, people want to be listened to, understood, respected, and served. They want a pleasant, stress-free purchase, and they want a service experience in comfortable surroundings. Should you surprise and delight them with these things, not only will you foster a loyal business relationship, your enterprise will flourish as they enthusiastically recommend you to their friends and neighbors.

If you're looking for customer service tips and techniques, don't read this book. But if you're seeking a practical, powerful plan that produces profitable results for your people, your customers, your community, and your company, then enjoy this book, use this book, and implement a servant's heart in your organization.

-Ben Novello
 Past President, Outback Steakhouse

Introduction

The Leadership Parable

Once upon a time, there was a CEO of a family-owned insurance company. He was the leader of a group of people who came to work every day and wanted to do a good job for themselves, for one another, and for their community.

Of course, not everyone had good intentions. They were just like any other company, with staff members who were lazy, who wanted to dump their responsibilities on other people, and who tried to manipulate the system. But the overwhelming majority of this company's employees were committed to getting the job done and doing things right. All they needed was a leader to show them the way.

When Frank Marshall became CEO of this company, he had no prior executive leadership experience. The highest position that he had ever held was as director of a claims department in a competitor's organization. He came from a large, well-known family in the community, and he had a lovely wife and four children.

When Frank was named CEO nearly five years ago, word spread quickly among the two hundred and fifty staffers at the Credibility Insurance Company. Feedback was very favorable, and there was plenty of optimism that Mr. Marshall would be able to build upon the strong foundation that the company's family owners had labored to establish over the past sixty-five years.

Corporate optimism grew to a fever pitch when, on his first day as CEO, Frank called a company meeting to outline his goals and to announce that he was keeping the organization's senior leadership team intact. This made everyone feel secure and hopeful.

For several months after that inaugural meeting, things appeared to be moving in the right direction. Sales were up four percent in a very competitive market and within a challenging economy; expenses were holding their own. Mr. Marshall made his rounds throughout the company at least once a week, asking questions, joking with the staff, and thanking his employees for their hard work.

Frank relied upon the senior staff that he retained to bring him up to speed on the various duties and responsibilities that came with being CEO of Credibility Insurance. He especially relied upon the company's Controller, Barbara Levinson. Ms. Levinson had been Controller for sixteen years, and she had functioned as CEO while the search for Mr. Marshall was underway.

Given all of this, it was a little surprising that, after eighteen months of relative optimism, there began to be increasing rumors and rumblings about Frank and his leadership style.

Frank seemed to be transitioning from the friendly, "new kid on the block" executive to a command-and-control type of leader who had lost passion for his people and relied more and more on the power of his office to get things done. Fading into the sunset were the days of supportive messages like, "Is there anything I can do to help you today?" With increasing frequency Frank's orders were, "You need to get this report out today, no questions asked."

During the following year, a few managers in key positions left the company, as did members of the rank-and-file. The percentage of turnover was increasing at an alarming rate, while customer satisfaction scores dipped below industry expectations. Never in the sixty-five-year history of Credibility Insurance was performance this poor or morale this low. It was awful. Managers bickered with one another and interdepartmental cooperation ground to a halt.

The beginning of the end of Frank's tenure as CEO came on June 3rd, the day that Barbara Levinson asked for a special meeting with the owner in order to submit her resignation. Immediately after speaking with the owner, Mr. Lenk, and his wife, Barbara said her good-byes, and with tears in her eyes she thanked everyone for the support that they had given her over the years. She then left for an extended vacation with her husband.

It was eerily quiet in the office for about a month after Barbara resigned. Frank tried to cheer everyone up with his plastic smiles and handshakes, but nobody was buying. The nail in Frank's corporate coffin came at a manager's meeting one day when he had the audacity to blame Barbara for the past year's dips in sales and customer service numbers.

After their early retirement many years ago, Mr. Lenk and his wife had seldom come to the office. While they maintained ultimate control of the business, they trusted the day-to-day operations of the company to the CEO and his staff. There was not an employee at Credibility Insurance who didn't love Edward and Anna. Both were genuine servant leaders and deeply respected for their integrity.

On July 8th, right after the holiday break, Mr. and Mrs. Lenk scheduled a company-wide meeting with mandatory attendance for all employees. After assembling in the company conference center, everyone stood up and applauded when Edward and Anna entered the room.

Edward escorted his wife to her chair and then approached the podium to speak:

First of all, I want to thank each and every one of you — most of you I still know by your first names — for being here today and for what you accomplish for our company on a daily basis. I appreciate you more than you know.

I'm here this morning to tell you that Frank Marshall submitted his resignation to Anna and myself at dinner last night. I want you to remember Frank for the enthusiasm that he brought to Credibility Insurance during his early months, and not for the most recent decline in our performance and morale. Frank and his family are good people. I take full responsibility for the pain you've recently experienced.

In fact, I apologized to Frank last night for not sharing with him as a new CEO the most important ingredient for executive success, and that is having a servant's heart. In addition, I never coached him along the way.

Today, I am here to apologize to you, to ask for your forgiveness for a bad decision that I made, and to join with me in moving forward from here and reclaiming what has always been the hallmark of our success, serving one another and our community.

For the next several months, Anna and myself will be on the premises every day, serving you, and charting a new course for our company as we search for a leader with a servant's heart. God bless you and thank you.

You would have to know Edward and Anna Lenk to understand why there was not a dry eye in the room after that brief message. But there was a loud standing ovation at its conclusion as well as a renewed sense of hope.

Introduction

Eventually, after listening carefully to the people who made their company successful, the Lenks found a new CEO who did have a servant's heart, and they returned to being one of the most legendary family-owned insurance agencies in the country.

So what's the meaning of this parable? Actually, it's the premise for the book.

The legacy of our family and of the Dimmitt Automotive Group is founded upon a single fundamental and family principle. Each one of us, by virtue of our intellect, emotions, and will, is endowed with the ability to grow and to develop a servant's heart. And to the extent that we are willing to take the risk of vulnerability that is associated with serving others, we will develop characters and companies that honor our families, our associates, our guests, and our communities.

That is our mission and our purpose as a family and as a company. Enjoy the book.

After moving to Clearwater from Georgia in 1924, Mr. Lawrence Dimmitt Sr. purchased the Ford dealership, located at the corner of Drew Street and Garden Avenue at that time. He traveled to different areas of the county, offering both fresh fruit and Ford vehicles for sale. Here, Mr. Dimmitt (in the light suit with tie) poses with his staff for a photograph in the 1920's.

Embracing the Brand

As automobile dealers, we are proud to represent some of the world's greatest automotive brands. The men and women of our industry gladly wear jewelry, ties, and pins that demonstrate that pride as they attend various events and conduct their day-to-day business affairs.

While enthusiastically supporting our manufacturers and their products, it became apparent to us that we needed to identify and develop the Dimmitt Automotive Group brand. We wanted our associates, our guests, and the community to know exactly who we are, what we stand for, and how we're going to support and grow our relationships within the community.

Simply stated, the term *brand* refers to the personality that identifies a product, service, or business. The experiential aspect of a brand represents all of the points of contact that a customer has with a company. We refer to that aspect as the *brand experience*.

During our new associate orientation at The Dimmitt Center for Learning, we invest time talking about our brand experience. In doing so, we begin by reviewing three important distinctions.

First, our instructor will ask, "If I mentioned the term *facial tissue* to you, what's the first thing that comes to your mind?" Nearly everyone in the class mentions the Kleenex brand. That instant brand recognition is often referred to as "top-of-mind" brand awareness. An individual may know nothing else about Kleenex, other than the fact that it's a tissue product that they have seen or used.

Then the instructor will inquire, "If I mentioned Tag Heuer to you, what's the first thing that comes to your mind?" There is a hesitation in the room, and after a few minutes someone says, "Watches?"

There's no doubt that this response would be quicker if each participant were presented with a list of watch manufacturers like Rolex, Swiss Army, and Movado. If they had access to such a list and recognized Tag Heuer as a watch, we would call that recognition "aided brand awareness." In other words, the brand itself wasn't easily recognized, but with the help of a list of watch brands, it was readily identifiable.

At the Dimmitt Automotive Group, however, we're not trying to achieve top-of-mind brand awareness or aided brand awareness. Our primary focus is to develop what is known as "strategic brand awareness" among dealerships in our industry.

Here is how strategic brand awareness might apply to Kleenex, for example. When the term *facial tissue* was mentioned in a conversation, a person loyal to the Kleenex brand might say, "Oh yes, Kleenex ... They have several different designs for the bedroom, bathroom, living room and even the garage. The tissues come in many different colors and they even have holiday-themed boxes." As it unfolds, that individual's knowledge of the Kleenex product would be a testament to the loyalty that they demonstrate to the brand.

It is that level of strategic brand awareness that we want to achieve in our organization. When people think of automobile dealerships, we want them to think "Dimmitt Automotive Group."

Our earnest desire is to have people view us as more than a business that sells and services cars. Of course, we want to provide the most reliable transportation possible for the people who place their trust in us. But we also want to be known for what we achieve for our associates, our guests, and our community.

When people think of us as a brand, this is the perception that we would like them to form: "The Dimmitt Automotive Group not only sells and services cars, but they really know how to serve others. Their staff relentlessly pursues excellence in creating the ultimate guest experience, and their beautifully appointed facilities make your visit both enjoyable and relaxing. I never felt like I was visiting a dealership. I left the building feeling like a part of their family."

Any business can say *what* they want to do from a brand development perspective, but the bigger, more primary questions that have to be answered are: *"Why* does it matter?" and *"How* are we going to do it?"

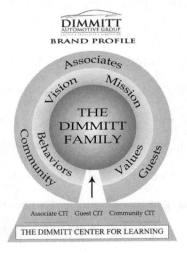

As you can see from looking at our brand development profile, everything at the Dimmitt Automotive Group begins with family.

Our family business legacy started in Savannah in the early 1900s. My grandfather, Larry Dimmitt, Sr., embraced his vocation in the automobile business by selling and servicing the Peerless car.

Before the turn of the century, my granddad participated in the Klondike Gold Rush and pursued careers in both the lumber and the railroad businesses. But it was the automobile enterprise that really captured his passion. Before settling in Clearwater, Florida in the early 1920s, he was associated with the Liberty car and the White truck. He was also the Buick distributor in the Georgia area and supplied sixteen dealers in that region.

When he arrived in Clearwater in 1924, my grandfather purchased a Ford dealership. He represented Ford and Lincoln until 1933, when he took over the sales and servicing of Chevrolet, Cadillac, and LaSalle.

For the next two decades, as the community of Clearwater grew and developed, my father, Larry Dimmitt, Jr., assumed the reigns of leadership from my grandfather. Nothing was more important to my grandfather and my father than establishing and growing a reputable business that served the needs of their community, while building that business on a foundation of trust, integrity, and respect.

In 1965, while our Chevrolet dealership continued to prosper at its original location, the family provided for a separate facility for Cadillac. In 1976, I purchased the Cadillac dealership from my father and became a third-generation dealer-operator.

It was 1986 when we relocated the Cadillac dealership to its current location in the Countryside area of Clearwater. Range Rover (now Land Rover), the luxury British four-wheel drive SUV, joined our Cadillac dealership in 1987 as the exclusive franchise on Florida's west coast and one of only twenty-five charter Land Rover dealers nationwide.

Presently, we have an area network of dealerships that spans Crystal River, Florida in the north to our Pinellas Park location in the south.

As we continue to grow and develop as a community partner, I'm blessed to have my wife, Doreen, and my two sons, Richard, Jr. and Peter, as integral parts of our mission to serve our associates, our guests, and our community.

We understand that those guests who purchase vehicles from us and drive them to our dealerships for service have families. The legacy that we've inherited from my grandfather and my father has taught us to care for those families, just as we would care for our own.

As you examine the Dimmitt brand profile, you can see that our family's mission is to be a role model for our brand image and to support our vision, mission, and core values. Through The Dimmitt Center for Learning, about which you will read later, we use continuous improvement teams as tools for ongoing personal and professional development.

Sir Richard Branson, Chairman of the Virgin Group, offered this thought about the significance of developing a successful brand: "Branding demands commitment; commitment to continual re-invention; striking chords with people to stir their emotions; and commitment to imagination. It is easy to be cynical about such things, much harder to be successful."

My father and grandfather were not opposed to hard work. They thrived on it as a matter of principle. Our family will continue to invest its energy in becoming better at what it does by serving those grandfathers, grandmothers, moms and dads, and children who reach out to us for assistance.

With thanksgiving and gratitude, we take pride in our brand. And we would like you to be proud of us as humble servants and dedicated professionals.

The infant days of the dealership on Ft. Harrison saw working conditions somewhat austere compared to today's high-tech facilities. Here, the dealership's 'technicians' take a quick break in this 1920's Service Department photo. The building was such that pigeons roamed and nested freely, and the roof leaked substantially every time it rained.

Our Mission

When we contemplated the manner in which we wanted to nurture, develop, and fortify our brand, we talked a lot about strategy, goals, and objectives, just as any healthy business would in the formulation of its operating structure.

Most importantly, however, we didn't begin there. As the noted author Stephen Covey recommends, we took our first steps "with the end in mind." We defined our vision, mission, core values, brand message, and core behaviors.

And we didn't just sit in our boardroom and make up a collection of words and phrases to impress people. No, we took a hard look at ourselves, established the importance of having a servant's heart, involved our associates in our thought processes, and made the decision not merely to sell and service automobiles but to make a difference in people's lives.

Therefore, it is with humble pride that we affirm the mission of the Dimmitt Automotive Group: *To improve the lives of our associates, our guests, and the community through service, excellence, and innovation.*

As noted anthropologist and author Simon Sinek writes in his book *Start With Why*, "People don't buy what you do; they buy why you do it." There is no shortage of automobile dealerships that sell and service vehicles quite successfully. It's not too difficult to determine what they do and how they do it. Nevertheless, it is not always crystal clear exactly WHY they do what they do.

Of course, if you ask business owners why they are in business, the customary response is, "We're here to make money." That's a given. Nobody starts a business to lose money. But isn't there something more? And how do you think consumers feel when they interact with an enterprise whose sole purpose is profiteering?

Don't get me wrong. There is nothing wrong with making money and operating a profitable organization. You cannot serve your customers effectively and

Our Mission

efficiently without being fiscally responsible and living on solid financial ground.

However, the *why* of the Dimmitt Automotive Group is founded upon corporate responsibility. As citizens of the community, we believe that, in addition to providing the best possible automotive experience for our guests, our purpose is to improve the quality of their lives.

The message that we want to communicate clearly each day to our associates, to our guests, and to the community is that people are our most important concern. Families matter to us. Somebody's husband, wife, mother, father, daughter, son, grandmother, grandfather, aunt, uncle, friend, or neighbor drives every vehicle that we sell and service. Their safety and satisfaction constitutes the rationale that they rely upon to determine their future interactions with our company.

When it comes to our mission as a company, the bottom line is that we don't want to conduct a transaction-based business where nameless faces purchase and then service the products that they buy from us. We choose instead to have a relationship-based company where people that visit us are treated like family and are cared for with the respect and dignity that they deserve, both now and in the future.

In the early days of Clearwater, there were very few miles of paved road, thus inspiring the "'scuse our dust" motto on the Ford's wheel cover in this 1920's photo. Mr. Dimmitt, Sr. hoped Clearwater could be the next Palm Beach...so much so, he eventually became a subsequent owner of the first house on the north end of the beach.

Our Values

*I*f the mission of an organization speaks to its purpose and why it is in business in the first place, then the core values of that company will define exactly what it needs to do in order to accomplish that mission. At the Dimmitt Automotive Group, we have defined three core values that drive our behavior on a daily basis.

Character

The legendary UCLA basketball coach John Wooden offered sage advice when he wrote, "Be more concerned with your character than your reputation, because your character is what you really are, while your reputation is merely what others think you are."

When we examined all of the possible core values that make our organizational mission a living, vibrant statement of our daily purpose for being, the value of *character* ascended to the top of our list.

Ever heard of Gus Hertz? Probably not. He was vacationing in the St. Petersburg, Florida area from Roanoke, Virginia when he found himself in a position to save three lives in two days. The 37-year old witnessed a driver who had a diabetic episode and drove his car into the Intracoastal Waterway. Hertz hurried to pull the victim from the submerged vehicle.

The next day, while fishing near the Sunshine Skyway Bridge, he watched a plane crash into the water only a few hundred yards from his boat, and he rushed to the rescue of the pilot and his passenger.

On both occasions, Hertz left the scene quickly to avoid the spotlight, and only later did he modestly claim responsibility for his heroics. While he easily could have called 911 and left the rescue to the first responders, he made a choice to act. In two moments of crisis, this person of character made a difference.

While the average person may never have two consecutive days of extraordinarily heroic opportu-

Our Values

nities, each individual experiences many occasions when character defines his or her purpose and path in life. Helen Keller said it best when she wrote, "Character cannot be developed in ease and quiet. Only through the experience of trial and suffering can the soul be strengthened, vision cleared, ambition inspired, and success achieved."

In the automotive business, we are faced with making tough decisions on a daily basis. In our efforts to do the right thing for everyone, it is virtually impossible to please every guest in every circumstance. Therefore, when making business decisions that impact people's lives, we rely heavily upon our vision, mission, and core values to arrive at the best decision, albeit not always the most popular one.

Our world is not just about the color of a vehicle that appeals to you, or whether or not you need a tire rotation with your lube, oil, and filter change. The type of relationships that we build and how we use our talents and abilities to strengthen and encourage one another defines both our individual and corporate characters.

Therefore, our Community Values Day and our Community Team Values Day make up a very important part of the foundation of our business operations. Each one of our associates who chooses to do so receives one paid day each year to volunteer their time to a not-for-profit charity in the Tampa Bay region. In addition, one day each quarter, a team of volunteers from the Dimmitt Automotive Group partners with other community organizations to volunteer for a special charitable event.

There is no question that participation and involvement in projects of this nature give our people a fresh and unique perspective about what really matters in life. Furthermore, as a result of their engagement with these community charities, they come back to work with renewed servant's hearts.

Martin Luther King, Jr. expressed a wish for his family that offers a clear picture of what a healthy society would look like. "I have a dream," he said, "that my four little children will one day live in a nation where they will not be judged by the color of their skin, but by the content of their character."

Our Values

The content of our character at the Dimmitt Automotive Group is rooted in our desire to serve our fellow citizens and, through our service, to be a hope and a help to them.

Commitment

Legendary football coach Vince Lombardi offered a timely observation about the power of commitment when he said, "Once a man has made a commitment to a way of life, he puts the greatest strength in the world behind him. It's something we call *heart power.* Once a man has made this commitment, nothing will stop him short of success."

Because commitment is one of our three organizational values, we also believe that when obstacles and challenges come our way, the *heart power* to which Lombardi referred will prevail and help us to attain both our business and cultural goals.

The automotive climate is extremely competitive. With numerous dealerships in a small geographic area, consumers have the power of choice to satisfy their transportation needs. Therefore, nothing less than a one hundred percent commitment from every associate on our team can enable us to rise above our competition and become the dealership of choice in our community.

The attitude that says, "Well, I showed up for work today—isn't that enough of a commitment for you?" just doesn't cut it in today's marketplace. If Steven Stamkos puts his uniform on for the Tampa Bay Lightning and just sits in the locker room, what can he accomplish? He has to get on the ice, skate into the corners, fight for the puck, score goals, and support his teammates. He gets sweaty and sometimes bloody, but at the end of the game, win or lose, he knows that he gave it his all. That's commitment.

At the Dimmit Automotive Group, commitment means the following things:

- √ Living our mission statement and core values every minute of every day.
- √ Doing whatever it takes to provide personalized, caring, and compassionate service to our guests and our community.
- √ Taking the initiative to support our fellow associates and leaders.

Our Values

- ✓ Internalizing the spirit of our guest service standards and living them on a daily basis.
- ✓ Doing whatever we need to do as leaders to serve our associates in the accomplishment of their work responsibilities.

The name Narayanan Krishnan probably isn't listed in your smartphone contacts. Everyday at about four in the morning, Narayanan wakes up, cooks a hot meal, and travels approximately two hundred miles to feed four hundred homeless people in Madurai, Tamil Nadu.

What is so interesting about Narayanan is that he had an award-winning career as a chef with a five-star hotel chain. On a visit to a Madurai temple, however, he came across a destitute man who was living in deplorable conditions. That frightful sight changed Narayanan Krishnan forever and it created within him a heartfelt commitment to serve his fellow man.

Seldom will we be faced with a dramatic incident that causes us to forge such a new commitment in our own lives, but the opportunities that we have in our business to positively impact countless lives on a daily basis is no less meaningful.

Race car legend Mario Andretti had this to say about the importance of giving total focus in the pursuit of excellence: "Desire is the key to motivation, but it's determination and commitment to an unrelenting pursuit of your goal — a commitment to excellence — that will enable you to attain the success you seek."

Not only is commitment a critical core value by which we can gauge our future success as a company, commitment is also an investment of faith that we make on a daily basis to those whom we serve.

Cooperation

The late Orison Swett Marden, founder of *Success* magazine, said this: "No employer today is independent of those about him. He cannot succeed alone, no matter how great his ability or capital. Business today is more than ever a question of cooperation." Cooperation is the core value that makes it possible for us to come together, stay together, and work together.

Our Values

Automobile dealerships are notorious for having been viewed as a collection of independent silos; we have a sales department, a service department, a parts department, a finance and insurance department, an accounting office, an Internet department, and a body shop. In the old days, cooperation was not always the rule of thumb when it came to interdepartmental relationships.

A customer drives into the service reception area promptly at seven o'clock in the morning to have a part installed on his vehicle that he ordered two weeks ago. He comes to find out that the part was out-of-stock and needed to be back-ordered, but no one in the parts department notified the appointment scheduler or the service consultant.

When the mistake is finally discovered, the message that the customer receives is, "I'm sorry, Mr. Smith. No one in the parts department told me that your part needed to be back-ordered. If they had told me, we could have called you and avoided this inconvenience. Now we need to schedule you back for another appointment."

Not only is Mr. Smith upset because one silo isn't talking to the other, but he is not exactly inspired when he finds out that the dealership that is supposed to help him doesn't actually communicate all that well with itself. In fact, it's embarrassingly obvious that the "blame game" is operative in the dealership when this service consultant throws the entire parts department under the bus.

Silos do not work in today's business economy. Dealerships are only as strong as their weakest link. Therefore, at the Dimmitt Automotive Group, we place a heavy emphasis on interdepartmental cooperation. We understand that in an era when time demands are paramount and service is king, customers don't really care whose problem it is that a part was not ordered. They measure performance by results. And the only way to achieve positive results is to have a staff that serves one another first and takes personal responsibility when things go wrong.

In our business, potential customers regularly come to one of our dealerships looking for a sales associate with whom they may have spoken months ago. The customer obviously remembers more about the vehicle in which they were interested than he or she does about the name of the salesperson who was of initial assistance.

To foster cooperation and integrity among our sales staff, the salesperson that greets the returning customer at the door routinely checks our Customer Relationship Management (CRM) system to determine who assisted that individual several months earlier. This accomplishes two things: it preserves the integrity of the working relationship among sales associates, while at the same time demonstrating to the guest the high level of cooperation among staff members.

There is no better description of what can happen to a group of people that does not cooperate and work together as a team than the one offered in this poem by an unknown author:

The Cold Within

Six humans trapped by happenstance
In black and bitter cold.
Each one possessed a stick of wood
Or so the story's told.

Their dying fire in need of logs,
The first woman held hers back.

For on the faces around the fire,
She noticed one was black.

The next man looking cross the way
Saw one not of his church,
And couldn't bring himself to give
The fire his stick of birch.

The third one sat in tattered clothes,
He gave his coat a hitch.
Why should his log be put to use
To warm the idle rich?

The rich man just sat back and thought
Of the wealth he had in store,
And how to keep what he had earned
From the lazy, shiftless poor.

The black man's face bespoke revenge
As the fire passed from his sight,
For all he saw in his stick of wood
Was a chance to spite the white.

And the last man of this forlorn group
Did nothing except for gain,
Giving only to those who gave,
Was how he played the game.

The logs held tight in death's still hands
Was proof of human sin.
They didn't die from the cold without.
They died from the cold within.

The famous British logician and philosopher Bertrand Russell once said, "The only thing that will redeem mankind is cooperation." Because we are all in need of redemption in every walk of life and in every business setting, cooperation is an extremely significant core value for us at the Dimmitt Automotive Group.

The Pledge

*I*n our company, we don't make promises that we cannot keep. Most customer service researchers tell you that making a promise to a customer and then not delivering is the equivalent of corporate suicide when it comes to reputation management and long-term guest loyalty.

Nevertheless, despite the common sense approach of "doing what you say you're going to do," today's marketplace is saturated with merchants who mistakenly believe that today's customers are not sophisticated enough to see through the smoke and mirrors and the fine print.

At each one of our campuses, we proudly display a pledge that is clearly visible to all of our guests. It occupies an entire wall in our dealerships, and it can be

The Pledge

found on every sales professional's desk. These commitments were not found in any book and no business professor framed our thinking. Instead, we sought the input of the people who actually do the work — our associates. We asked them what they thought mattered most when it came to executing our mission to improve the quality of life of those people who visit our family. This is what they said:

Our pledge
we will listen
we will learn
we will stay late
we will show up early
we will strive to exceed your wildest dreams
we will make mistakes, and correct them to the best of our ability
we will do whatever it takes to deliver a legendary customer experience
we will always be there for you
thank you for allowing us to serve you today
your Dimmitt *Family & Friends*

So what's the difference between a promise and a pledge? From our perspective, a *promise* refers to a specific behavior or act, whereas a *pledge* is a commitment to a code of conduct, a way of life.

When we are establishing and enriching our associate, guest, and community relationships, we cannot rely upon a promise to always "do the right thing," for example, or to be fair and honest. How a business wants to conduct itself has to be defined, spelled out, and articulated in a simple and straightforward manner, using language that engages everyone.

At one of our campuses, an attorney in his mid-forties who was also a new guest looked at our pledge in the service department waiting area. He approached one of our associates nearby and inquired as he pointed to the pledge, "Are you really going to do this for me?" Our associate replied, "Oh yes, sir, I know that we will." The attorney then recalled the blockbuster movie *Field of Dreams*, starring Kevin Costner. Against all odds, Costner's character builds a baseball field in the middle of nowhere, and cars begin to line up for miles just to see it. The attorney said, "There was a line from the *Field of Dreams* movie ...

The Pledge

'If you build it, they will come.' Well, if you actually do what you say you are going to do in that pledge on the wall, customers will be lined up for miles just to get in your dealership because no one else behaves that way consistently."

We intend to do just that. When you look at our pledge, read it a few times, and absorb its true meaning, you will discover that we are not doing anything extraordinary or unusual. We are merely pledging to treat our guests in a manner that dignifies and honors their trust and confidence in us.

Servant Hearts

In 1931 the Ford and Lincoln dealership was moved to 603 South Ft. Harrison, and in 1933 Mr. Dimmitt, Sr. took over sales and servicing of Cadillacs, LaSalles and Chevrolets. Lawrence Dimmitt, Jr. took over from his father in 1952. Mr. Dimmitt, Jr. (left) is pictured with his parts truck in front of the Ft. Harrison location during the mid 1950's.

Developing the Right Leaders

Three of the things about which employees most often complain are a lack of openness, a lack of honesty, and a lack of trust in their relationships with their employers. In the majority of situations, they form their opinions about these qualities by looking to their leader or immediate supervisor.

The work environment at some businesses gives customers the impression of a well-oiled machine with outstanding morale, yet inside team members suffer in silence until they can't take the phoniness or office politics anymore. Then they leave.

Weak managers mask this problem by hiring even weaker associates, and a progressive, downward spiral continues until the ownership steps in to reclaim control of the business.

In order to avoid mistakes in recruiting, selecting, hiring, training, and promoting leaders, it is incumbent upon CEOs to internalize those qualities that produce organizational results while at the same time creating an environment of openness, honesty, and trust. An executive who can do this is the type of leader who will grow your company.

Those leaders have five fundamental traits, the first of which is:

The right leader connects as well as communicates.

Former General Electric CEO Jack Welch once said, "Any company trying to compete … must figure out a way to engage the mind of every employee." That engagement or connection begins with the company's leaders.

When communication becomes more than merely the dissemination of information, this is because legendary leaders have connected with their employees. When interdepartmental communication transcends individual differences and personal agendas, legendary leaders have connected with their employees. And when businesses enjoy a sustainable competitive advantage in the marketplace, this has happened because legendary leaders have connected with their employees.

The second fundamental trait is:

The right leader creates passionate empowerment.

Perhaps the most recognized leader for creating passionate empowerment in the work setting was Herb Kelleher, the former CEO of Southwest Airlines, who built that company with what he referred to as "integrity, guts, and nuts." At Southwest Airlines, every employee has been entrusted with fulfilling the company's mission. "We've never tried to be like other airlines," Kelleher said. "From the very beginning we told our people, 'Question it. Challenge it. Remember, decades of conventional wisdom have sometimes led the airline industry to huge losses.'" If a policy, procedure, or practice appears to be in conflict with Southwest's mission and corporate values, employees are encouraged to voice their opinions and concerns. They're empowered to think like owners and to make decisions that are consistent with the organization's larger objectives.

In a similar fashion, Herb Kelleher will always be idolized for shaping a passionate culture where risk taking is encouraged. When it comes to taking care of the customer, Southwest Airlines has discovered that passion, and not technique, is the foundation of legendary service.

During a magazine interview, Kelleher once described a practice that is certain to foster a healthy work environment: "I can't anticipate all of the situations that will arise at the stations across our system. So what we tell our people is, 'You handle them the best way possible. You make a judgment and use your discretion. We trust you'll do the right thing.'" It's no surprise that empowering employees the way Herb Kelleher did went a long way toward establishing Southwest Airlines as a company with legendary service. It is also one reason why Southwest receives thousands of job applications every year and hires only a fraction of these applicants. Though once you're hired, you're part of the family.

The third fundamental trait is:

Real leaders celebrate the power of teams.

Synergy is the collective energy of a group of people that is more powerful, more potent, and more productive than the energy of just one person. When synergy exists within an organization, the results are impressive.

For nearly two decades, Cadillac and General Motors have advocated the use of continuous improvement teams in their dealerships, and we've embraced that initiative wholeheartedly. Cross-functional groups of our associates come together to study our processes and various aspects of our business and to make recommendations to improve our performance. No one has the market cornered on great ideas, so we always look to our staff for new and creative approaches to organizational improvement.

The late psychologist Ernest Becker wrote this in his Pulitzer Prize-winning book, *The Denial of Death*: "People are capable of the highest generosity and self-sacrifice. But they have to feel and believe that what they are doing is truly heroic, timeless, and supremely meaningful." Leaders who support continuous improvement teams in their organizations accrue the benefits of the generous and self-sacrificing employees who buy into meaningful corporate goals and objectives.

The fourth fundamental trait of good leadership is:

Real leaders persevere against adversity.

In today's turbulent economic times, perseverance is a priceless commodity. When you get knocked down, you have to stand up, brush yourself off, and get back into the game. History is replete with stories of people who gave us great examples of perseverance.

"Rudy! Rudy! Rudy!" The cheers in Notre Dame Stadium must have been deafening when Rudy Ruettiger entered the game against Georgia Tech one October day in 1975. The Fighting Irish created a legend when Rudy, the kid who was too small to play college football, became the only player in Notre Dame history to be carried off the field after a game. The entertaining movie *Rudy* depicted the life of a young man whose perseverance against all odds made him into a living legend.

Perhaps the greatest example of American perseverance can be found by studying the life of one of our country's most revered presidents, Abraham Lincoln. Having endured political defeats, failed businesses, the death of his fiancée, and a nervous breakdown, Lincoln managed to shape the destiny of the United States of America forever.

Is there a common thread that binds together the perseverance that is displayed by leaders from all walks of life? What all great leaders possess is a refusal to fail. These men and women do not give in to the limitations that have been imposed upon them by others. Albert Einstein characterized the struggle to persevere by saying, "Great spirits have always encountered violent opposition from mediocre minds." Legendary leaders know that when mediocrity says, "You can't," perseverance says, "I can."

The fifth and final fundamental trait of good leadership is:

Real leaders behave according to a personal code of conduct.

One of the best ways to maximize leadership potential is to evaluate your behavior on a regular basis. And a personal code of conduct is a terrific tool for doing just that. A personal code of conduct will help you to examine how you think, feel, and act, and it can give you direction to do the right thing. Codes of conduct are nothing new. There's the Ten Commandments, the Boy Scout Oath, and the American Serviceman's Code of Conduct, just to name a few. It was the poet Ralph Waldo Emerson who urged us to "go put your creed into your deed."

Recalling once again the esteemed UCLA basketball coach John Wooden, when he graduated from elementary school, his dad gave him the following seven-point plan to guide his future actions:

1. Be true to yourself.
2. Make each day your masterpiece.
3. Help others.
4. Drink deeply from good books.
5. Make friendship a fine art.
6. Build a shelter against a rainy day.
7. Pray for guidance and give thanks for your blessings daily.

Wooden always said that this code was one of the most powerful and long-lasting influences on his life. And can anyone argue with his success? People who develop and internalize similar codes of conduct benefit from established parameters of right and reason.

Holocaust survivor Viktor Frankl wrote, "Evermore people today have the means to live, but no meaning to live for." A personal code of conduct is an affirmation of what matters to us as people and as leaders. It's a daily reminder of what we need to do to strengthen our relationships with our families, friends, and colleagues.

Hiring The Right People

When they're thinking about the staffing needs for their companies, most executives have been urged at some point to make sure that they "get the right people on the bus." Of course, that's easier said than done, especially in our complex marketplace and challenging economic times.

The owner of a small, growing company was preparing to put an advertisement in the newspaper and online for several job openings within his organization. The business coach who was advising the owner made a case as to why this was not such a good idea. "Do you really want to recruit people that are looking for *jobs*?" asked the coach. "I don't think you want job-hunters coming to work for you." The owner was perplexed. So the coach went on to say that people looking for jobs are typically dispassionate about the businesses that hire them. Those employees come to work, fulfill their responsibilities (for the most part), get paid, go home, and care little about the long-term success of the company for which they work. They are vested financially and that's about it.

"Oh, so you're telling me that I need to find people who want a career," queried the owner. "Not necessarily," the coach said, "because I have seen my share of disengaged and frustrated doctors, plumbers, salespeople, and engineers, and they all had careers."

At this point, the owner became demonstrably upset. "OK, if I'm not looking for people who want jobs or careers, then exactly what am I looking for to help grow my company?"

"Simple," replied the coach. "You need to be looking for people who have a *vocation to serve*, people who feel that it's their calling to serve their co-workers and your customers. You need to be searching for people with a servant's heart."

At the Dimmitt Automotive Group, we want associates who know what it means to serve one another, our guests, and their community. A willingness to serve tells us that a potential associate has a strong character, excellent self-esteem, and the potential to engage others in a manner that enables them to achieve their personal dreams and professional goals.

The Walt Disney Company not only understands the concept of a servant's heart but has mastered it to the point where its philosophy of hiring "cast members" for attitude and training them for skill has earned them success beyond measure. They create happiness for people of all ages everywhere.

As I noted in the last chapter, if we are going to have a company that is populated with servant's hearts, it makes perfect sense that we also need servant leaders. The late Robert K. Greenleaf, the undisputed father of the Servant Leadership movement, had this to say:

A new moral principle is emerging which holds that the only authority deserving one's allegiance is that which is freely and knowingly granted by the led to the leader in response to, and in proportion to, the clearly evident servant stature of the leader. Those who choose to follow this principle will not casually accept the authority of existing institutions. Rather, they will freely respond only to individuals who are chosen as leaders because they are proven and trusted servants. To the extent that this principle prevails in the future, the only truly viable institutions will be those that are predominantly servant-led.

As we continue our exciting journey to tomorrow, the hallmark of our success will be founded upon our willingness to enthusiastically serve one another and our community. Therefore, "getting the right people on the bus" means finding those who have a vocation to serve, and then creating a work environment that encourages them to employ that gift of service.

At one point, Larry Dimmitt, Inc. provided a number of unique services tailored to seasonal customers, including long-term rentals and warehouse vehicle storage. This photo, probably taken around 1940, shows the original building on Ft. Harrison and the new car lot, as well as the billboard and a print ad explaining our innovative services to seasonal visitors.

The Language of Loyalty

Once the right leaders are in place and the right people are on the bus, it becomes important to discern the difference between a *customer* and a *guest*. Trust me, not many companies get this.

A friend was dragging his suitcase, briefcase, and a six-pack of Diet Coke into a hotel one August night. As he approached the front desk with an enthusiastic, "Hi, I'm Tom Joseph," the clerk raised his eyes from the newspaper that he was reading and said, "Checkin' in?"

Relishing the opportunity to have a little fun in response to such a ridiculous question, Tom said, "No, I'm here for the hockey game." Without blinking an eye, the clerk replied, "Can we keep the same credit card on file that you used to make your reservation, and how many keys would you like for your room?"

The clerk wasn't even listening to my friend. He was merely moving his lips onto the next line in his script. Needless to say, Tom told me that he would not be staying at that hotel again.

Oh, the pretenders talk a good game about how "the customer is #1" and how "we love our customers like family," but the tragic truth is that talk is cheap, and many businesses today are outrageously clueless when it comes to comprehending the true language of loyalty. Only when corporate leadership understands the dynamic difference between a customer and a guest can long-term loyalty and profitability in the marketplace be achieved.

Customer	*Guest*
Transaction	Relationship
Need	Want
Conquest	Invitation
Expense	Investment

When we think of a customer today, the word "transaction" comes to mind. A customer buys groceries at the grocery store. Customers pay bills, make appointments for service, and get coupons in the mail for discounts to their favorite restaurants.

After their transactions are complete, they might receive a survey to fill out so that the business can understand these customers' level of satisfaction with the product or service. If the customers' transactions don't measure up to their expectations, they quickly take their business elsewhere. On the other hand, most companies never bother to survey their customers because, quite frankly, they don't really care about anyone's opinion, good or bad.

When we think in terms of guests and not customers, what we perceive primarily is a relationship. And the relationship that characterizes a guest coming to your place of business is founded essentially upon trust and respect, rather than on money or merchandise. You cannot buy trust and respect with a coupon or a flyer that discounts your automobile, television, or meal. Guests are too savvy and sophisticated to be duped by sales gimmicks, bait-and-switch techniques, and downright unethical manipulation.

Another fundamental difference between a customer and a guest is that while a customer may need to get his or her automobile repaired at your dealership, a guest wants to come to you for help. And no one can put a price tag on what the difference between a need and a want means for your bottom line.

Statistics from consumer research groups around the country indicate that people who want to do business with you because of your trust and respect profile are 77% more likely to develop a long-term relationship with your business than those who merely need your product or service. Show me a CEO who is not interested in that type of loyalty.

Also, we often hear the term "conquest" used when businesses target a group of people whom they want to expose to their product or service. I don't know about you, but "conquest" creates visions in my head of being attacked on a showroom floor by a crazed salesperson who cuffs me, blindfolds me, and drags me into an office until I sign on the dotted line. Thankfully, of course, that salesperson manages to offer me a bottle of water on the house.

Companies that want to be successful have to cross over the chasm that separates customer conquest and acquisition from guest invitation and investment. Let me ask you a question: Do you genuinely care about the people who come to your house because they saw the sign on the corner or in the newspaper for your Saturday garage sale? I didn't think so. But when you've cleaned your home, prepared a nice dinner for your invited guests, thought about how you can serve and entertain them, and then welcomed them in with a handshake, a hug, or a smile, that's a different feeling, isn't it? Truthfully, it's no different in business. Most of us know when we're being "sold" as opposed to communicated with. Good businesses communicate with us by means of their appearance and their behavior that they value our presence and that they're willing to satisfy our wants, both today and in the future.

What is problematic is the warped thinking that a customer is actually perceived as an expense in the corporate minds of most companies. And because businesses are customarily conditioned to cut expenses, what they mistakenly do is diminish the experiences of potential consumers after they've spent thousands of marketing and advertising dollars to get them there in the first place.

Let me give you an example of what it means to diminish the experience of a potentially long-term consumer, and then another example of how to properly invest in the guest experience in order to achieve the type of loyalty that results in more permanent relationships.

A friend of mine, Terry, visits a periodontist for gum surgery. The receptionist does a wonderful job arranging the appointment and confirming that Terry has the correct pre-surgery medication and instructions and that he is at ease about the procedure. When he arrives at the office, Terry is greeted by the dental assistant who reviews what will happen for the balance of the appointment, answers any of Terry's questions, and makes him as comfortable as possible. The doctor's engaging personality makes him feel confident and the procedure is completed without incident.

However, as Terry is preparing to leave, he is detained by the office manager who indicates that she has not been able to verify his insurance coverage and implies that he may have been at fault in providing her with inaccurate information.

Everything gets resolved after a couple of weeks but what Terry remembers, of course, is the unpleasant encounter that he had with that office manager who wanted to speak with him after his gums had just been cut open and sewed back together. As a result, his experience as a first-time guest at the periodontist's office was considerably diminished, despite the evident care and compassion of most of the staff.

In another instance, a mom drove her luxury SUV into a dealership for an emergency tire repair with her three-year-old son. As the service consultant approached the vehicle and began to seek the opinion of his technician, both of them noticed that the mother's boy was crying and upset because he left his favorite teddy bear at home.

After the tire had been repaired and the woman and her son were escorted to their vehicle, this mother was shocked to see that someone had placed a brand new teddy bear on the rear seat. Needless to say, her son had a big grin on his face as he hopped into the vehicle and embraced his new friend. Now what kind of impact do you think a $10 investment in a teddy bear had upon the mother of that little boy from a guest experience perspective?

For those who trivialize the importance of how we employ language to communicate with consumers, the word "customer" seems to be a good enough description for any person who purchases our goods and services. Despite the popularity of that term, however, embracing the powerful difference between a customer and a guest is both non-negotiable and requisite for any knowledgeable leader whose mission it is to apply the language of loyalty and to engage an invited group of potential consumers who have expressed an interest in developing long-term relationships with the business.

Larry Dimmitt, Jr. (second generation owner) took over the business from his father in 1952. When this picture was taken around 1960, we had several satellite used car lots throughout Pinellas County. In addition to the Cadillac and Chevrolet franchises, Mr. Dimmitt also owned several rental car companies which helped supply the satellite lots with inventory.

Guest Service Standards

*M*ahatma Ghandi once said, "The best way to find yourself is to lose yourself in the service of others." There's a lot of wisdom in those words and once we have understood the difference between a customer and a guest, the concept of "losing ourselves in the service of others" can inspire us to define specific standards of behavior within our organizations, standards that can be applied to the ways that we treat one another as well as the ways that we treat our guests.

Rather than adopt complicated behavioral formulas that are nothing more than psychobabble, we've implemented the following six common sense principles to guide our everyday interactions with our guests:

1. Extend a warm welcome and greeting to every guest.
2. Take the initiative to make eye contact and smile from the heart.
3. Create opportunities for guest engagement and listen with empathy to their needs.
4. Use appropriate body language during all interactions.
5. Employ the LAST (Listen, Apologize, Solve, and Thank) approach for service recovery.
6. Sincerely thank every guest and extend a cordial invitation to return.

It's our belief that when our associates internalize these behavioral objectives and demonstrate them in their everyday interactions, both the work and the guest environment can energize people and create an atmosphere of mutual respect and trust.

To say that our guest service standards are unique or are better than the standards of conduct that have been embraced by other legendary service companies would be untrue. We studied how Disney, Ritz Carlton, Southwest Airlines, and other companies routinely treat their customers, and we hope that our approach will enable us to mirror their high levels of customer satisfaction success over time.

Guest Service Standards

In years past, you could walk into a retail merchant and ask to be directed to its customer service department. At the Dimmitt Automotive Group, that office doesn't exist. In our dealerships, customer service isn't a department; it is everyone's responsibility to take the initiative to care for each and every guest who visits.

Initiative is the key concept that drives our guest service standards. The attitude that often undermines most attempts at creating a positive guest service environment is the thought, "If someone needs my help, I'll be glad to help them." The same thing happens with the Golden Rule: "Do unto others as you would have them do unto you." The Golden Rule doesn't mean, "Well, if he's nice to me then I'll be nice to him." Just as the Golden Rule begins with a verb, legendary guest service begins with taking the initiative to engage co-workers and guests rather than waiting for them to ask for assistance.

Henry Ford once said, "Coming together is a beginning. Keeping together is progress. Working together is success." At the Dimmitt Automotive Group, we want to come together in support of our guest service standards; we want to let our common initiative serve to keep us together in the accomplishment of our mission, and we want to work together for the ongoing benefit of our associates, our guests, and our community.

In 1960, as now, one of the highlights of the showroom was a hand painted mural. The impressive showroom was a significant landmark along Ft. Harrison for more than five decades.

Respect

The late Rodney Dangerfield made a living with his self-deprecating comedy by lamenting, "I get no respect, no respect at all." Of course, if Rodney had been an associate at the Dimmitt Automotive Group, he wouldn't have had any material for his act, because he'd get more respect than he ever dreamed was possible. Respect is an essential ingredient in our guest service standards. Without it, nothing that we do to achieve our mission makes any sense.

Of course, the word "respect" has so many different applications that it's important to understand its meaning in terms of what we are trying to accomplish within our dealership family. For our associates, guests, and the community that we serve, respect means that we value, honor, and celebrate their dignity as human beings. We do that by engaging our people with a servant's heart and by responding to everyone's needs and concerns with compassion and competence.

It's no stretch of logic to conclude that respect is what distinguishes a healthy workplace from an unhealthy one. Take a look at these two environments. I'm certain that you'll discover where respect most certainly resides.

Healthy Workplace	**Unhealthy Workplace**
Great productivity is present.	It is difficult to get things done.
Employees feel empowered to do their job and suggest improvements.	Employees feel powerless to change the way things are.
People enjoy working together and associating with their co-workers.	There is a climate of unfriendliness and gossip.
Challenges and obstacles are discussed openly with managers and employees.	Challenges and obstacles are acknowledged but not discussed.

Everyone is willing to help when needed.	"It's not my job" is heard routinely.
When mistakes are made, employees are coached in performance improvement.	When employees make mistakes, they are criticized and ridiculed.

When one reviews the significant distinctions between healthy and unhealthy workplaces, it becomes obvious that respect is an essential element of an environment where an energetic spirit for service yields positive outcomes for everyone.

The German philosopher Immanuel Kant urges us to "always treat people as ends in themselves, never as a means to an end." There is no question that one of our everyday key behaviors should be to treat every associate and guest as the most important person who we'll meet that day. When we extend ourselves to others in that manner just one time, the benefits come back to us a hundredfold.

Servant Hearts

When this photo was taken about 1962, the dealership had just expanded to give Cadillac and Chevrolet their own showrooms. The large building in the background on the right is the Ft. Harrison Hotel, built in 1926. Still a prominent landmark in Clearwater's skyline, the hotel, like Dimmitt Cadillac, has weathered the many physical and economical challenges of the 20th century.

Trust

*E*rnest Hemingway wrote the profound sentiment, "The best way to find out if you can trust somebody is to trust them." There is a wealth of wisdom in that statement, yet trust is often misunderstood in relationships of every kind.

At the Dimmitt Automotive Group, not only do we want our guests to trust us with their transportation needs but we want them to feel confident that our mission is to improve the quality of their lives as well.

Similarly, it's our desire to provide a work environment where associates collaborate in a spirit of teamwork that is built upon a foundation of trust.

While we represent various manufacturers that produce quality products, our guests purchase their vehicles from us and service them with us. They place their trust in our company to deliver an automobile that provides safe and reliable transportation for their family and friends.

Only a shortsighted dealer principal believes that his or her company is in business to sell or service cars. Today's consumer expects more. The dealer who has earned the trust of the community is destined to achieve a sustainable competitive advantage in his or her city or town.

Who wants to do business with someone whom they don't trust when there are many opportunities to engage with trustworthy merchants who sell the same product or service? Who wants to work for a dealer who doesn't foster a climate of trust in the workplace?

Last year, a major national research company interviewed thousands of U.S. workers about their experiences at their jobs. Their conclusions highlighted an "erosion of trust." One of the statistics in particular was startling. They found that less than 12% of those surveyed believed that their employer genuinely listened to and cared about its employees. My question is, "What kind of guest service do you think the other

88% are delivering to those who visit their places of business?"

When pressed for the reasons behind this erosion of trust, the researchers identified four principal explanations:

1. Poor communication
2. Lack of perceived caring
3. Inconsistent behavior
4. Perceptions of favoritism

At the Dimmitt Automotive Group we believe that we can create trust in the work environment by expecting our managers to be servant leaders. We regularly ask our associates questions like, "Is there anything that I can do to help you to accomplish your tasks at work today?" or "How can I better serve you as your manager and coach?" and we're confident that a "servant leader coach" is the type of manager that can develop the talents of our people while at the same time fostering trusting relationships.

No one can put a price tag on trust. When it's present in relationships with employees and customers, its value is immeasurable. When trust is absent, however, the financial and emotional consequences can be devastating.

When a newborn gazes into the eyes of his or her parents for the first time, the trust that one human being places in another frames an entire lifetime. At the Dimmitt Automotive Group, we believe that our vocation is to nurture that trust in the lives of our associates and guests and invite that trust forward as we carry out our guest service standards.

Flashy posters adorned the windows of the original Cadillac/Chevrolet showroom on Ft. Harrison. Even into the early 1960's, the dealership actively marketed its rental car program.

Being Genuine

A commentator on a national network thought that the person whom he was interviewing about a court case was being deceptive in response to his questions. After the interview had concluded and while the microphone was still running, the commentator was heard expressing his frustrations to the cameraman: "Do you think that there are any genuine people left in this world?"

Do you need a lesson in what being genuine is all about? Spend some time observing and interacting with children in preschool. They are the exact opposite of some of the more counterfeit and plastic personalities that haunt too many commercial establishments today. I listened to a three-year old in the mall who was upset with his grandmother for wanting to leave the play area.

With a stern look and folded arms, he glanced up and said, "I'm not happy with you, Grandma!"

Unfortunately, people at work don't always communicate with that level of honesty. What they customarily do is to express their displeasure to another colleague or supervisor, thereby creating a network of gossip and innuendo without addressing the problem at hand.

In a business setting, employees develop with reasonable clarity an opinion about whether or not their boss is genuine. And a majority of customers is quick to pick up on whether or not an employee is genuine. Hiring and retaining disingenuous leaders and employees is one of the cardinal sins of organizational development.

When Meridian was transferred to a new department so that she could supervise a staff of thirty employees in the call center of a major telecommunications company, she inherited a highly productive and efficient staff whose most recent supervisor had been forced to resign in order to care for a sick family member.

Things went well for the first two or three months before there were some offsite emails and social media postings concerning Meridian and her department. Not only was the high morale and camaraderie slipping, the department's productivity wasn't the same.

Several more weeks passed and Meridian was scheduled for a two-week vacation. During her absence, the area manager, whose leadership credentials were impeccable, covered the office. While Meridian's employees were reluctant to complain about her and the area manager didn't undertake a fishing-for-information expedition, it became obvious that there were problems.

It turned out that when disgruntled customers contacted the call center for assistance, Meridian had developed an internal team of about a half-dozen "go to" people to handle the most irate callers. And while that may not be a bad idea on paper, the manner in which this internal team was formed and the way in which it was communicated to the balance of the staff left those who were not selected to feel inferior and incompetent.

While Meridian was displeased with the way some of the troubled callers were handled, she never brought her concerns directly to the team and never once coached her staff members about opportunities for improvement. For these reasons, the majority of the people in the call center lost respect for Meridian and felt as though she was not being genuine.

As an acquaintance of mine reminded me long ago, "You only have one chance to make a good first impression." The same is true of being genuine. The one time that you're not genuine, you take the risk of being permanently perceived as disingenuous.

Just as important as trust and respect are to the successful execution of our guest service standards, being genuine in your everyday behavior and interpersonal relationships is the key to expressing the power of your servant's heart.

Though they still retained some vestige of their aero-styled, daring design of '59, when this photo was taken in 1965, Cadillacs had become more streamlined and conservative.

Compassion

There's much to be learned from the lives of those who leave this world prematurely. Rachel Scott was seventeen years old when she became the first victim of the Columbine High School massacre in 1999. Before she was murdered, Rachel wrote, "Compassion is the greatest form of love humans have to offer."

Compassion in the service business implies not merely an awareness of the concerns, misfortunes, or distress of others, but an enthusiastic willingness to reach out and help to alleviate these troubles whenever possible.

One of our technicians was driving home from work in the early evening when he noticed a vehicle pulled off to the side of the road with its flashers blinking. Rather than relaxing after a hard day in the garage and enjoying a leisurely ride to his house, he pulled up in front of the car and offered to assist the distraught woman behind the wheel. Within a short time, her minor problem was resolved and both parties were on their way to their respective destinations.

Maybe it doesn't sound like a big deal to take a few minutes to help a stranded motorist. But that example of compassion in action is exactly what we must do with greater frequency as we endeavor to serve the families of our community by ensuring their safety and security.

Every year in the automotive industry millions of dollars are spent by dealerships on customer acquisition campaigns, yet very few dealer principals are routinely ecstatic with their results. It seems to me that our marketing and advertising initiatives would be a lot more effective if compassion became the main guideline for establishing customer rapport. As we attempt to navigate the traditional "road to the sale" that's always been taught to sales professionals, maybe we should pave that road with compassion for those who have traditionally viewed the act of buying a car as a punishment rather than a pleasure.

Compassion

It's gratifying to hear the joy that associates tell me they experience when compassion is freely bestowed upon our guests. This has me convinced that all of the marketing and advertising dollars in the world can't buy the type of loyalty that compassion earns us as a business.

George Washington Carver said, "How far you go in life depends on your being tender with the young, compassionate with the aged, sympathetic with the striving, and tolerant of the weak and strong. Because someday in your life, you have been all of these."

As we continue to grow and build our family of associates, we will continue to look for those who are blessed with a compassionate heart and who understand the importance of what it means to really know, to engage, and to uplift those guests who come to us for help. This is the way that our company chooses to do business.

Change

*I*n commenting on the power of one individual to effect meaningful change, Mother Teresa said, "I alone cannot change the world, but I can cast a stone across the waters to create many ripples." This astute insight reflects well what we're trying to accomplish on a daily basis for those whom we serve. Change is not only a fact of life; it is an absolute necessity when it comes to managing a company that relies upon the trust and confidence of both its employees and its customers.

We don't sell and service vehicles the way it was done last year, five years ago, or decades before. We don't wait for the manufacturer, the media, or automotive analysts to tell us how we should serve our customers and consumers. No, our goal is to be pioneers when it comes to anticipating the needs and desires of our people, our guests, and our community and then to respond with a servant's heart in a manner that addresses each of their concerns.

No one can deny that technology has dramatically impacted the way that vehicles are sold in America. We are interacting with a more knowledgeable and sophisticated buying public in the twenty-first century. They understand vehicle pricing, product features, and financing options, and they can test-drive and build the vehicle of their choice online. And their most precious commodity, of course, is time.

In addition, increasing numbers of consumers have no interest at all in visiting the showroom. They want the vehicle to be brought to their homes or places of business, and if you can bring lunch, well, that would be good too. While they might be impressed that you can deliver their vehicle using the most current tablet technology, what are you going to do to impress them tomorrow?

For better or worse, the idea of a sales manager that you see in television advertisements—he pounds the hood of car on his lot and promises to beat the competition—is repulsive to most people today. The simple fact is that change in our world and in our industry is necessary for ongoing growth and development. A part of our brand development as a company is to anticipate, understand, and respond quickly and maturely to the changing demands of our marketplace.

Today, vehicles do not only take you where you want to go. They can verbally guide you to your destination, offer music and restaurant suggestions, and provide cameras that direct your every move and sensors to let you know when another car is too close. And that's just to name a few features. Because automobiles have changed and because the behaviors of consumers have changed, successful dealerships are part of a never-ending process of change as well.

Despite all of the change in the business world, however, one thing will always be constant within our company. We will always take care of our guests in the present, while searching for innovative ways to improve their experiences with us in the future.

The Dimmitt Center for Learning

For as long as I can remember, we have sent our associates to the numerous training programs that are sponsored by the manufacturers that we represent as well as some provided by outside vendors. Our people also invest valuable time completing online courses in order to satisfy various sales and service certification requirements.

However, as we prepare to meet the evolving demands of the consumer as well as respond to the educational needs of those who join our family of associates, the importance of Peter Senge's "learning organization" has made us want to strengthen the education and training that we provide to our people. It was Senge who said, "The only sustainable competitive advantage is an organization's ability to learn faster than the competition." Therefore, to accelerate our efforts to learn and to adapt to the needs of our associates, our guests, and our community, we established The Dimmitt Center for Learning.

The driving force behind The Dimmitt Center for Learning is a board of trustees comprised of ten of our associates who manifest the core values and behaviors that we embrace as we continue to grow the Dimmitt brand. These ten trustees come from both of our campuses and from every department in our company.

While this board of trustees constitutes a strategic arm of our organization, four cross-functional continuous improvement teams offer ongoing suggestions to our leadership team as to how we can improve both our people and our processes as well as find better ways to serve our guests and our community. When a continuous improvement team is tasked with a particular topic that impacts the guest experience, for example, they come back to the board of trustees and the ownership with a solid and rational implementation plan for their recommendations. During their weekly meetings, the continuous improvement team considers these questions in the preparation of their report:

> *How important is this topic to the health of our company?*
>
> *What are the obstacles that we have to address in order to make progress?*
>
> *What specific outcomes are we trying to achieve?*
>
> *From whom do we need to get buy-in to address these issues successfully?*
>
> *What will life be like here when this topic is addressed positively?*

While a continuous improvement team typically consists of between five and eight people, it's our goal to reach 100% participation among associates in the not too distant future. No one has a monopoly on good ideas or the correct way to do things. What we are discovering is that, as we mine the talents of our people in a number of areas and implement the recommendations of our teams, we achieve buy-in to their ideas and solutions more quickly and more enthusiastically.

Furthermore, the collaborative nature of a cross-functional continuous improvement team lends itself to enriched organizational communication overall, as well as a willingness to reach out across departmental lines and solve the minor, daily challenges that all businesses face in a positive and non-confrontational manner.

As we continue to grow The Dimmitt Center for Learning, it is our vision to partner with the local academic community to offer a variety of seminars and symposiums for the benefit of families and businesses in our region.

One of the incontrovertible laws of human nature is that, to the extent that you give to others what they want, they will give to you what you want. In creating The Dimmitt Center for Learning, we want to give our people an opportunity to develop their talents and skills and to become the people and professionals whom they are capable of becoming.

We have found that as we give our people this opportunity, they reward us each day and a hundred times over by reaching out with their servant's hearts to be a hope and a help to those whom they encounter on our campuses.

The Dimmitt Center For Learning

During the late 60's and early 70's, Larry Dimmitt, Jr.'s brother-in-law, "Uncle George" Sanders, managed the Cadillac franchise when it was moved for a few years to a temporary location downtown on Cleveland Street. The Chevrolet store eventually moved onto Cleveland Street, and Cadillac expanded on Ft. Harrison to two showrooms and a pre-owned lot.

Service in America Today

*E*ven with a core structure in place that is founded upon a solid mission and a series of core values, before we can assess our performance or measure our success, it's important that we understand what's happening in our country relative to taking care of customers.

Customer service in America today leaves a lot to be desired. Other than a sprinkling of legendary companies across the country, most businesses either just don't get it or they just don't care. After examining the current state of customer engagement in our nation, we can see five distinct levels of service quality.

Level 1: We're going out of business soon.

It's almost hard to believe that these types of establishments open their doors each day. In the case of a restaurant at Level 1, there's no greeting at the door, you have to wait to be seated, and the server approaches you by saying, "Have you made up your mind yet?" After you place your order, it takes forty-five minutes to get an appetizer and your soup is cold by the time that it arrives. You would complain, but now you can't find the server. The whole experience is a disaster.

To make matters worse, just before you doze off while watching the late night news that same evening, you notice that the restaurant where you had attempted to impress your girlfriend is featured on a special episode of "Dirty Dining" because of the roach problem that it's having in the kitchen.

Eventually—and thankfully—many of these businesses close voluntarily or are put out of their misery by a regulatory agency.

Level 2: We believe that mediocrity is our friend.

The mediocre enterprise is just that—mediocre. It opens its doors in the morning and closes them in the evening. In between, nothing extraordinary happens. Customers come and customers go, and the job gets done with little fanfare and no major complaints.

If the mediocre business was a greeting card shop, you wouldn't get much more than your cards. No one would ask you if you needed help in selecting anything special. The cashier would scan your cards and tell you how much you owed, and you would be on your way out the door. Of course, the fact that you were interested in a small gift to go with the card that you purchased would have escaped the hourly high school student employee who was doing her homework at the cash register while you shopped.

Level 3: We're trying every day.

Level 3 companies comprise the greatest volume of service businesses. They will usually give you a smile at the door and ask you if you need anything else before you go. The company might sponsor a local soccer team, and if a customer has a complaint, it eventually gets resolved.

For the most part, people are satisfied with the service that they receive from Level 3 businesses, although their services are more transaction-based than relationship-oriented. These businesses are more interested in getting the job done than they are about caring for their customers in any genuine sense.

Profit is the end result for these numbers-driven organizations, and they're reasonably successful at maintaining the status quo. Level 3 businesses are vulnerable, however, when the economy is fragile, or when their competition wants to move to a higher service level.

Level 4: We take service seriously.

Making it to Level 4 is a very promising beginning for companies who truly understand the importance of providing great customer service. The main separation between a Level 3 and Level 4 service provider is the difference between a company that is interested in merely conducting a transaction versus one that is committed to establishing long-term relationships.

A dental manufacturer of crowns and implants, a family-owned enterprise, had been in business for about forty years. They had grown over time from the three brothers who founded the operation to a small company of about thirty people.

The brothers had a simple philosophy that they learned from their parents. Simply stated, they did whatever it took to satisfy their customers. After they developed a strong customer base in their local community, dentists from around the country began to contact them. They had an opportunity to sell their business along the way, as well as a chance to expand to an even greater volume of clients. They chose to do neither. For them, the niche that they had established enabled them to earn a handsome profit while completely satisfying their customers.

The average length of employment for their thirty employees was twelve years. Five of these thirty non-family staff members had been there from the beginning. Morale was high and collaboration was the rule of thumb.

The three brothers were heavily involved in their churches and their community, and their personal and professional reputations were impeccable. They firmly grasped the reality that when you put people and their needs first, good things happen for you and your company.

Level 5: We live service as an art form.

When you're at the highest level of customer service, people talk about you, write about you, and come to visit you so that they can harvest your ideas and apply them to their own companies.

Everyone has heard of legendary service champions like Ritz Carlton, Disney, and Southwest Airlines. They're so well known and highly thought of that other companies make large investments of time and money in order to send their employees to them for classes and seminars.

But you don't have to be a hotel, a theme park, or an airline to make service an art form. You also don't have to be perfect. Ritz Carlton, Disney, and Southwest Airlines will all tell you that they have unhappy customers from time to time. This is just human nature and it is virtually impossible to please all of the people all of the time. Having said that, when a business makes it to Level 5, customers rave about their guest experiences and they become advocates for the company.

Service as an art form just doesn't happen miraculously. Level 5 businesses separate themselves from the pack of pretenders through the commitments they make to "getting the right people on the bus" as well as ongoing employee training and development. When you realize that one employee's telephone call, tone of voice, posture, appearance, or response to a request can make or break your company's good intentions, then

Servant Hearts

training and accountability become the brushes that you use to paint a masterpiece of legendary service.

A part of that training is developing and understanding the six roadblocks that impede the expression of legendary customer service. That's what we'll review in the next chapter.

During the early 70's, the leadership helm passed to Larry Dimmitt III. While the Cadillac dealership was still in its temporary location on Cleveland Street, it started a revolutionary (for its time) program of quick oil changes. It was at this point in Clearwater history that commerce was beginning its move away from the heart of downtown.

The Six Roadblocks to Legendary Service

*I*n order to reach Level 5 where service is an art form, it's necessary to avoid the six catastrophic roadblocks that can derail your progress in a heartbeat.

Roadblock #1: Apathy

It doesn't take long to figure out that some employees just do not care. And it's not that they are having a bad day, or that there is something bothering them at home, because we all experience those life events.

Normally, a company does not hire an apathetic employee unless it is fooled during the job interview. Apathy is like a germ that gradually infects peoples' attitudes until they couldn't care less about helping or being nice to anyone.

Let me give you an example of apathy in action. Shopping for a shirt and a tie, an elderly gentleman is the only customer at a small men's store at the mall. Behind the cash register, a young man reads a magazine as he waits for the next guest to check out. Not once does he ask the elderly gentleman if he needs any help or if he requires a particular shirt size. Furthermore, as a chime sounds to announce that another guest has entered the store, the clerk raises his eyes briefly and then goes back to reading his magazine. That's apathy.

Roadblock #2: Dismissal

Have you ever been brushed off or dismissed by an employee? "I need to do a couple of things and then let me get to you" is a typical comment from someone who does not know how to properly greet a customer.

The dismissal usually occurs when disgruntled customers want an explanation of a particular issue or a resolution to their problem. Because that may interfere with a current sale or require some extra effort, the employee dismisses the guest, placing him or her in the cycle of "when I have time for you, that's when I'll be ready to help you."

Of course, no one likes being brushed off or dismissed, and this only complicates future attempts to assist the guest. And with the time demands that most people face today, a temporary dismissal on the part of one employee can mean a permanent good-bye from that customer.

Roadblock #3: Coldness

There's no excuse for this roadblock. Being cold to a guest or potential customer is a death knell for future business. Why would anyone want to patronize a business where legitimate questions have been treated with a curt, cold response? Sad to say, even when a customer leads with an emotionally vulnerable statement, an employee's response can often be less than friendly.

Very recently, a woman purchased a large refrigerator for her home and within a month of the purchase, her husband died unexpectedly. The refrigerator was much too big for what she needed on an ongoing basis as she learned to live alone, so she went back to the appliance store in search of relief.

After she had explained to the store manager that her husband had recently passed away and that she had financed an appliance that she didn't need anymore, let alone afford, the manger — without even expressing sympathy for the woman's loss — said, "You'll need to contact an attorney if you have one; there's nothing we can really do for you at this point." Does it get any colder? Even if nothing could have been done under the circumstances, the woman just told the manager that she had lost her husband. How much effort would it have taken to offer a little compassion and sympathy?

Roadblock #4: Condescension

Employees with the lowest levels of self-esteem often fall prey to the roadblock of condescension. Because they don't feel very good about themselves, they make it a habit of trying to ensure that their customers feel as bad as they do.

A customer purchased a beautiful, 60-inch flat panel television from a major retailer near his house. When he took the television home, he realized that he still needed a few more questions answered about the operation of certain features on the set.

Realizing that the floor model that he had seen at the store on his initial visit was the same model as the one he ultimately purchased, he went back to the business for another tutorial. The salesperson who sold him the television had left for the day, so he approached another associate for assistance. When he asked his questions, the salesperson said, "Didn't you get a manual with your television? If you took the time to read and understand the manual, you wouldn't have had to waste your time coming back here."

Obviously, making customers feel inferior doesn't exactly create repurchase loyalty.

Roadblock #5: Robotism

When employees become robots at work, they aren't much fun to encounter. They never allow any divergence from the established routine, and they don't want anyone to challenge the robot's authority.

Waiting to board a flight on a major airline, a passenger made the mistake of attempting to claim his coach seat through the First-Class/Preferred line, even though his section had already been called for boarding. When he approached the airline representative to hand her his boarding pass, she said, "This lane is for any first-class passengers who may not have boarded yet. You have to go back and around the chain, and then board through the coach section."

Another customer was uncertain about a warranty claim benefit, so she called the manufacturer's help line for assistance. When a representative took her call, the customer indicated that she had two questions that she wanted to ask about the warranty. The representative told her that because of the high volume of calls that day, he would only be able to answer one of her questions.

While robots do exactly what they are told to do by their supervisors, their rigidity creates hassles for customers who are longing for a little common sense.

Roadblock #6: Run-Around

When customers complain about merchants, it's common to hear the expression "they're just giving me the run-around." We've all been there at some time or another.

When customers experience this roadblock, it is usually for one of two reasons. First, the company may be too focused on making sales to new customers instead of keeping the ones it already has. Second, the company may be failing to create customer-friendly processes that make it easy to do business with them.

A customer who bought a computer was entitled to a rebate by using a coupon that was given to him at the time of his purchase. Following the directions that he had been given, he mailed in the rebate offer with a copy of the receipt as well as the barcode from the product's box. The rebate did not come within the promised time period. After three months, seven telephone calls, and one letter of demand from an attorney, the customer finally got his check. Do you think he will be buying anything from that manufacturer again?

It is our intent to remove as many roadblocks as possible and to create a user-friendly environment for our guests. By creating a stress-free shopping and buying experience, we hope to solidify the trust that our customers place in us as we look forward to long-term relationships with them.

Overcoming Negativism

William James, the Harvard psychologist, made a powerful statement that has been quoted by counselors for years: "If people could only realize that by changing the inner attitudes of their minds that they could change the outer aspects of their lives."

The amount of negativity and cynicism in the workplace today is crippling the performance and creativity of many businesses. And while these attitudes are typically directed toward various people, places, and things, they are born of the beliefs of each individual human being.

The antidote to all of the negativity and cynicism that permeates our world is to first understand one's "negative self-scripts," and then to build toward a more positive approach to life, family, and work.

What are negative self-scripts?

➢ Negative beliefs that you have about yourself—for example, "I can't do anything right."

➢ Negative descriptions given to you by your family of origin or peer group when you were younger and that you still embrace today—for example, "You are so lazy that you'll never amount to much."

➢ Negative feedback that you have received from your boss, spouse, co-workers, or others that you have taken personally and incorporated into your personal belief system.

➢ Negative assessments that you or others have made about your competency, skills, ability, knowledge, intelligence, creativity or common sense—assessments that you have come to believe internally.

➢ Negative attitudes about your possibilities for achievement or success in life; these influence your motivation, effort, and drive toward the attainment of your goals.

What is the outcome of believing these negative self-scripts?

- Over-dependence on the approval of others.
- Lack of self-worth and low self-esteem.
- Negativism, pessimism, cynicism, and self-pity.
- Depression.
- Fulfillment of the prophecy and buying into the patterns of self-destruction.
- Immobilization. A rigid belief system immobilizes you and prevents you from taking risks, freezes your feelings into a negative pattern, and convinces you that your only role in life is to be victimized by those from whom you cannot escape.
- The "Guard-All Shield." You create an invisible shield that is tough for others to see or to penetrate. People approach you at work with a comment or suggestion, but you zap them away with your shield and they back off. This shield can be so subtle that the person using it may not even know it exists. It takes the form of coldness, wisecracking, aloofness, fear of failure, or any other feeling that keeps you from connecting emotionally with another person.

Overcoming our negative self-scripts isn't easy. It's the responsibility of the leaders in our organization, as it should be in any company, to constructively challenge negativity and cynicism whenever they raise their ugly heads. Permitting these attitudes to pollute even one person or department can lead to a corporate illness that has no miracle cure.

Individual employees can overcome their personal negativity and cynicism by employing a process of self-affirmation and thereby develop their full potential as human beings. Becoming a self-affirming human being and a productive employee at work implies a threefold process that involves the internalization of three key concepts:

1. *I am*: This is a statement of who you are, a positive affirmation of a real state of being that exists within you. You can create a full list of "I am" statements by taking a personal, positive inventory of your attributes, strengths, talents, and competencies. Examples include: 'I am talented'; 'I am generous'; 'I am a competent sales associate'; 'I am trustworthy'; and 'I am an efficient and effective service manager.'

2. *I can*: This is a statement of your potential, a positive affirmation of your ability to accomplish your goals. It is a statement of your power to grow, to change, and to help yourself. "I can" statements assist in the development of short-term goals. Examples include: 'I can control my temper'; 'I can be honest with my feelings with my supervisor'; 'I can achieve certification as a master technician'; and 'I can laugh and have fun.'

3. *I will*: This is a statement of positive change that you will pursue, a positive affirmation of the change that you want to effect in your life. It's a success prophecy, a statement of what you want to accomplish both now and in the future. Examples include: 'I will manage my time better today'; 'I will praise my children today'; 'I will offer words of encouragement to my staff on a daily basis'; and 'I will face my challenges with courage today.'

The continual, daily use of internal statements like these is designed to counter specific negative self-scripts that diminish our personal success and productivity. A focus on developing oneself as a person will result in a positive attitude, reduced stress, a sense of optimism, and more self-motivation toward emotional growth and fulfillment.

From a work perspective, when this personal energy is translated into a "We Are, We Can, and We Will" approach to business, the probability of ensuring a sustainable competitive advantage multiplies exponentially.

Curing Corporate Cancer

*T*hus far, we've talked about the cultural alignment of our company as well as some of the challenges that businesses face in the current economy. In the following chapter, we'll begin a discussion of the importance of emotional intelligence and coaching in the pursuit of business goals.

Before that, however, it's necessary to address the silent killer that can wreak havoc on businesses and sends many of them to the brink of collapse and then over the edge of the corporate cliff.

It's dynamic. It's dangerous. And it's frightening. Q & S disease will blindside you, wrap its arms around you, and sack you for a devastating loss like a defenseless NFL quarterback. Telling yourself that your company doesn't have the illness is the worst form of denial, because you do. Every organization does. Some just learn how to manage it better than others.

The sad reality is that the symptoms of Q & S disease are black and white, measurable, and capable of being addressed and contained. Yet in many cases leaders don't even acknowledge them. Just like a person who knows that his high blood pressure may be leading to something more serious but ignores his doctor's recommended treatments, business leaders often refuse to tackle key indicators of Q & S disease like poor employee morale; decreasing customer satisfaction scores; sub-standard personal, team, and organizational performance; and eroding productivity, sales, and profitability.

In speaking with business executives and leaders about Q&S, I've noticed that they all understand it, but that less than twenty percent have any prior experience doing anything about it. What's even more tragic is that when they really do comprehend it, only a handful has the courage to deal with it. Almost no one wants to get up from the turf, shake off the sack, and run the next play in the never-ending battle against this dreaded opponent.

"Quit and Stay" disease is a company's worst nightmare.

Here's an anonymous, real-life scenario of how this illness unfolds in a typical company. Bob Miller worked in a sales organization that wanted to improve its performance, productivity, and profit. Bob was a professional in his forties and a likeable guy, and he had been with the company for a little over a decade.

Over the past five years, Bob's numbers had been trending downward, with poorer sales results each year as well as decreasing customer satisfaction scores. Despite his likeability factor, he looked unhappy and his co-workers seldom observed him smiling or interacting in a meaningful way with other staff members. Management had finally reached their wit's end with him.

In the middle of a one-on-one coaching session with an outside consultant, Bob was asked point blank, "When did you quit your job?" At first, Bob glared angrily at the consultant, didn't say anything, and put his head down on his chest. After a few seconds, however, he looked up and in an almost shameful whisper admitted, "Maybe five years ago."

Five years earlier, Bob Miller had disengaged from his company personally, professionally, and emotionally, but he hung around because the job market was dismal and he had nowhere to go. His survival instincts told him that he needed a paycheck, benefits, and a place where he didn't have to learn new products, processes, or procedures. This job was easy for him, even comfortable. So he QUIT his job and he STAYED with the company — a classic example of Q & S disease.

What the coaching consultant came to learn about Bob was that he was an exceptionally gifted and talented professional who had been passed over for a promotion to become a sales manager. The company negotiated its managerial selection process poorly, and Bob reacted to the rejection even worse. He became both a silent and vocal critic of the organization to internal and external customers. It was later discovered that while he sold at marginally acceptable performance levels, he was referring the customers whom he did sell to another location to have their products serviced.

When Bob's boss was asked why he was still there after five years of manifesting Q & S, he said, "Well, he sells a little better than our worst salesperson." If you can discover the wisdom in that statement, you have a better grasp of logic than I do.

There are Bob Millers in your company. For whatever reasons — and they are multiple, I promise — these people have quit their job but they're still there, collecting a paycheck and benefits, performing at or below minimally acceptable standards, and all the while sowing the seeds of discontent among your team members and customers.

These Bob Millers continue to work for you because you don't see how their behavior impacts your bottom line, because you see it and you don't know what to do about it, because you see it and you don't want to do anything about it, or because Bob Miller is somebody's relative or friend who needs a J-O-B.

You have a choice. You can be a haven for quitters and stayers and watch your business slowly evaporate, or you can learn to manage Q & S disease and work toward developing a sustainable competitive advantage in your market. If you decide to opt for the latter, you need to manage the health and profitability of your organization by doing these things:

- Survey your employees annually to discern their levels of professional and emotional engagement with your company. Then act upon the results of this survey as necessary.
- Make certain that you don't have any quit-and-stay leaders working for you. If the manager of one of your departments has quit and stayed, what type of productivity do you think you are getting from that person's employees?
- Define your vision, mission, and values and ensure that they are an integral part of your day-to-day operations. Hold people accountable for their behaviors and steer them toward behaviors that fortify your culture.
- Create a work environment where healthy and abundant communication negates divisive cliques, and where a manager's first responsibility is to understand and apply the principles of servant leadership with all of his or her employees.
- Get the right people on the bus. Develop a strong recruiting, selection, hiring, and training protocol and adhere to it religiously.

> Make sure that every employee has a coaching plan that encourages their development and growth in their career and vocation within your organization.

These few suggestions form the foundation for a game plan to minimize the impact of Q & S disease. The final recommendation requires a bit more explanation.

At least once a year, conduct a thorough, high-level review of your entire staff. Determine who your disciples are. These are the committed employees who are passionate about carrying out your mission with both dedication and enthusiasm. Acknowledge and celebrate their contributions to your company in meaningful ways.

Then determine who are your middle-of-the-road employees. These people get the job done, but their engagement with your vision, mission, and values is marginal. Create and execute a plan to coach and to challenge them in a positive manner in order to achieve higher levels of performance and then follow through with those plans.

Finally, identify those people on your staff who, for whatever reasons, have quit and stayed with your company. Constructively confront their behavior and invite them to re-engage with your business's vision, mission, and values. Should they decline that invitation in the coming weeks and months, then acknowledge their wishes and provide whatever outplacement services you deem appropriate.

The fact of the matter is that in these economic times, you can't afford to have quit and stay employees like Bob Miller collecting checks while contributing next to nothing to their co-workers and customers. It's just plain wrong. While Q & S disease will always be a part of the workplace, its effects can be conquered with leadership, due diligence, and appropriate and constructive interventions.

Coaching Is Key

When exit interviews are conducted with employees nationwide, some of the results shock business owners and executives. Of course, they're not too surprised to see "need better pay" listed as a reason for departure, but the one comment that always alarms them is, "I'm leaving because they never taught me anything."

Employees want more than to be paid fairly for their skills; they want to continue to learn, grow, and develop on the job. One of the greatest football coaches of all time, Lou Holtz, had this to say: "I won't accept anything less than the best a player's capable of doing, and he has the right to expect the best that I can do for him and the team." When the mangers and leadership in a business understand this, personal and organizational performance skyrockets.

Here lies the problem. Coaching in the workplace has taken a bad rap as being "soft" and having nothing to do with productivity. Throughout the years, five myths have arisen about why coaching may not be the best investment of a manager's time and energy.

Myth #1: *Coaching in the workplace cannot be accurately defined.*

Myth #2: *Some people just can't be coached.*

Myth #3: *Coaching is like mental health therapy.*

Myth #4: *A coach is nothing more than a cheerleader.*

Myth #5: *Coaching has nothing to do with improving the bottom line.*

At the Dimmitt Automotive Group, this is how we respond to those myths, one step and one day at a time:

Reality #1: *Coaching in our company is clearly defined.* For our leaders, there's no confusion about the definition of coaching. It involves a partnership between a leader and an associate that is characterized by two commitments. The leader commits to fostering an environment where each team member has an opportunity to learn, grow, and develop in his or her vocation. In a similar fashion, the associate commits to the development and implementation of a Personal Growth and Development Plan (PGDP), which is reviewed annually and used as a tool for ongoing coaching sessions throughout the year.

The PGDP identifies specific action steps that will be taken by the associate and supported by their manager for the purpose of achieving personal and professional job satisfaction, career development goals, and buy-in to the Dimmitt Automotive Group's vision, mission and values. That partnership begins, however, with a clearly defined process for recruiting, selecting, hiring, and training new associates. We have a user-friendly orientation process that starts with our Human Resources Department and includes a mentoring program for new staff.

In addition, each new associate participates in three hours of coaching and training with our Dimmitt Center for Learning instructors in order to acquire a thorough understanding of how our vision, mission, core values, and behaviors can contribute to the strengthening of a culture in which they can be proud to work.

Reality #2: *Any associate with an open mind and a willingness to learn, grow, and develop can be coached.*

The fact of the matter is that some people think that they have all of the answers. No one can tell them anything that they don't already know. This is not the type of person we look to hire for our staff.

On the other hand, to say that an individual cannot be a good sales or service consultant just because he or she has never been a sales or service consultant before is detrimental to finding a person with exceptionally great people skills, skills that might help this person to develop into one of your very best sales or service consultants.

Cadillac dealers had the good fortune of participating in a custom-designed training program at the Disney Institute in Orlando, Florida. At this session, the instructor was asked to explain what the Magic Kingdom looked for in potential cast members. The simple, straightforward response was, "We hire for attitude and we train for skill." That very successful philosophy affirms the importance of coaching for skill development, and we are committed to accomplishing this kind of coaching in our organization.

Reality #3: *Coaching in the workplace and mental health counseling are two different creatures.*

Let's be honest and clear. There are individuals working in every kind of business setting who are troubled with depression, anxiety, marital problems, and an assortment of unfortunate mental health issues. That's the nature of society. And that is why we afford our associates with the opportunity to avail themselves of professional counselors via our Employee Assistance Program (EAP).

However, coaching in the work setting has nothing to do with these mental health issues. Our efforts focus on three levels of skill development: people skills, process skills, and work-specific skills. With people skills, we're looking to strengthen areas like communication, guest service standards, and problem solving and conflict resolution strategies. When coaching for process skills, we pay close attention to understanding and preparing reports and leading effective meetings, for example. In the area of work-specific skills, we might focus on specific, manufacturer-required training for our technicians or a class in Microsoft Excel for our office staff.

Our hope is that when an associate leaves our employment, their reason for departure will not fall into that category of "I'm leaving because they never taught me anything."

Reality #4: *An inspirational leader is a lot better than a cheerleader.*

Everyone knows that cheerleaders hold rah-rah pep rallies and root their teams to victory. Inspirational leaders, on the other hand, prepare their teams, develop their teams' talents, and capitalize on each person's individual strengths while creating a commitment to common team goals.

The key to being that kind of inspirational leader in our organization is not giving great speeches or motivational talks. What we need from our team of leaders is to set the example for the type of service that we expect our associates to provide our guests. And setting the example means coming to work everyday with patience and humility and asking those people who report to you what you can do to serve their needs.

Reality #5: *Coaching has everything to do with improving the bottom line.*

The fact of the matter is that improved morale, lower employee turnover, associate buy-in to departmental goals, and better teamwork all have a substantial impact on an organization's bottom line.

There's no question that a positive mindset results in better individual and company performance in the face of adversity and challenges. The coaching of inspirational leaders contributes greatly to a positive climate at work. As a matter of fact, in a meta-analysis of over 200 studies on employee satisfaction and success in the workplace, researchers Sonja Lyubomirsky, Laura King, and Ed Diener found strong evidence of a direct connection between life satisfaction and successful business outcomes.

While these are the five most common myths about coaching in the workplace, one major shroud still surrounds the practice. Unfortunately, many employees at every level of an organization perceive coaching as a disciplinary action. Often, coaching is the first step of a very unpleasant three-step journey from coaching to counseling and finally to termination.

At the Dimmitt Automotive Group, however, coaching is the first step in bringing our vision, mission, and core values to life. While we do have a totally separate process for handling behavioral complaints and concerns, the coaching that we do is intended to minimize the likelihood that any individual will face a disciplinary proceeding.

In order for our positive coaching process to achieve its intended results, we make it clear to our managers in developmental sessions that there are five key coaching responsibilities that are a part of their mission as leaders.

Responsibility #1: *Every manager is responsible for creating a work environment within which associates can enhance their people-, process-, and work-specific skills.*

Responsibility #2: *Every manager is responsible for building a collaborative coaching relationship that is based upon mutual trust, transparency, and open communication.*

Responsibility #3: *Every manager is responsible for thoroughly understanding the character and competencies of team members so that he or she can guide those team members to higher levels of professional development and personal enrichment.*

Responsibility #4: *Every manager is responsible for applying the principles of emotional intelligence and for employing core-coaching competencies in order to maximize their effectiveness in the coaching relationship.*

Responsibility #5: *Every manager is responsible for developing his or her team members' belief in the value of the coaching relationship. As this belief is strengthened, each team member will feel more comfortable sharing their knowledge, skills, and abilities with both the coach and fellow team members.*

If coaching sounds like a lot of work to you, it is. While some businesses may be comfortable investing far less time and effort in their people, that's not our style. We believe that a solid coaching relationship between a manager and an associate yields multiple long-term benefits for the individual, for our guests, and for our community.

Emotional Intelligence & Coaching

You probably know at least one highly intelligent and gifted person who was promoted to a leadership position at work, only to become a colossal failure in a short time.

And you probably also are aware of someone with better-than-average, though not exceptional knowledge and technical skills who was similarly promoted to a leadership role in an organization and became extraordinarily successful.

Given the fact that different styles of leadership can be equally effective, it's fair to ask, what causes one leader to succeed and another to fail? Volumes of research support the theory that understanding the practical applications of emotional intelligence is the single most critical element that all effective leaders have in common, despite their diverse approaches to leadership.

As mentioned earlier, we expect leaders in our company to help their team members with skill development. But when emotions are involved, the task is a little more arduous. As Aristotle wrote about anger in his *Ethics*, "Anyone can become angry—that is easy! But to be angry with the right person at the right time, for the right purpose, and in the right way—that is not easy."

Of course, anger is just one of the many emotions that we can experience on a daily basis, so the question is whether or not managing those emotions constructively in the workplace is all that difficult. The answer: it's easier when you employ the principles of emotional intelligence.

Simply stated, emotional intelligence is a potent combination of self-management skills as well as the ability to collaborate with others. Contemporary research by professors at both Harvard and Yale appears to pinpoint five foundational elements of emotional intelligence:

> Knowing and understanding your emotions.
> Learning how to manage your emotions.
> Applying the principles of self-motivation to personal growth and development.
> Recognizing and understanding emotions in others.
> Managing relationships effectively.

In one of the landmark studies on emotional intelligence, Harvard University psychologist Daniel Goleman studied over one hundred eighty companies in order to determine which personal competencies drive outstanding performance within an organization. Goleman's study included three categories of competencies:

1. Purely technical skills, like re-building an engine or business accounting.
2. Cognitive abilities such as deductive reasoning.
3. Competencies illustrating emotional intelligence, such as the ability to work well with a team.

"When I analyzed all this data," Goleman concluded, "I found dramatic results. To be sure, intelligence was a driver of outstanding performance.

Cognitive skills such as big-picture thinking and long-term vision were particularly important. But when I calculated the rate of technical skills, IQ, and emotional intelligence as ingredients of excellent performance, emotional intelligence proved to be twice as important as the others for jobs at all levels." Goleman went on to say that emotional intelligence assumed an even more important role at the highest levels of these organizations, where differences in people's technical and cognitive abilities were negligible.

Goleman's study is only one of many that have been completed over the past three decades that underscore the power of emotional intelligence in the workplace. Therefore, it's important to take a brief look at each of those five foundational components of emotional intelligence and to learn how they can be applied successfully to our everyday relationships.

Knowing and Understanding Your Emotions

It's impossible to be completely effective in a coaching relationship without having a thorough knowledge and understanding of your emotions. It just doesn't happen.

Larry was the director of a hospital laboratory who had just lost his job. He was in shock after the termination because he'd always been told that he was one of the hospital's brightest administrators. The hospital dismissed him because the turnover rate in his department was twice the average of the other departments, and morale in the lab was at its lowest point in five years.

As it turned out, Larry was fired because he didn't know or understand how much the emotion of fear was destroying his leadership. He said that he'd been afraid of losing his job ever since he started working at the hospital. It had been his first leadership role in any organization, and he thought that if he and his team members could do everything perfectly, the payoff would be job security. As a result, Larry micromanaged his department to death, and his team members distanced themselves from him. No one on the executive leadership team really knew what was happening.

Larry's fear ultimately resulted in his dismissal. Why? Because fear had prevented him from becoming an effective coach for his people. In his mind, coaching meant over-controlling and stifling the creativity and enthusiasm of his staff.

While Larry's story is disappointing, it's a clear example of how critical it is to know and understand your emotions as both a leader and a coach.

Learning How To Manage Your Emotions

It's one thing to know and understand your emotions; it's another thing to manage them successfully. To fully grasp the transition between understanding and managing emotions, think of the angry samurai who got in the face of his Zen master and challenged him to explain the meaning of heaven and hell.

With a condescending tone the Zen master said, "You're nothing but a moron, and I can't waste my time with an idiot like you."

When he heard his character being assassinated like this, the samurai flew into a rage, drew his sword, and shouted, "I could kill you for your disrespect."

In a very gentle and unassuming voice, the monk said, "And that is hell."

Amazed at the wisdom of the Zen master, and seeing that he had been possessed by a violent rage, the samurai immediately stepped back, put away his sword, and thanked the master for his insights and bowed before him.

"And that," the monk replied in the same unassuming voice, "is heaven."

Learning how to manage your emotions does not mean finding a way to repress them. Rather, managing your emotions in a coaching capacity means using them constructively in order to bring out the best in your team members.

As you sit in a departmental meeting where one of your associates presents a thoroughly inaccurate report, you could bang on the table and knock things over, scream and yell at the group, or just sulk, not say anything, and get up and leave. Or you could manage your emotions by avoiding any hasty judgments, stepping back, considering the mitigating factors (including your own involvement, if applicable), selecting your words carefully, and offering a proposed solution to the problem.

By using the latter approach, you create a climate of openness, trust, and integrity in the work environment. Your associates will be able learn from their mistakes and you will give evidence of your levelheaded leadership, thereby fortifying the coaching environment.

When you think about it, there are three emotional positions you can take in life in any interpersonal situation:

1. *I will act the way I feel.* If you choose this position when you're having a bad day, your results will be no better than those of the samurai. In this position, emotions are king, and if the emotion is anger, resentment, impatience, fear, or frustration, odds are that you will do some damage with your words and actions and create relationship casualties along the way.

2. *You will act the way I feel.* Your emotions are still in control here, and in this position you choose to make others feel as miserable as you do. Recently I heard a manager at a restaurant say to his employee, "I'm upset so you should be upset too." Having your team members feel as miserable as you do is completely counterproductive.

3. *I can't help the way I feel right now, but I can help the way I think and act.* This position uses the very best blend of your three greatest resources as a leader and a coach: your intellect, your

emotions, and your will. If one of your team members mishandles a transaction with a guest in the service drive, you might manage your reaction by using this approach: "I'm so frustrated and angry with what I'm seeing and hearing, but working myself into frenzy at this point accomplishes nothing. What I need to do is express my concerns, coach the associate, and agree upon whatever steps are required to avoid this happening in the future." Integrating this third emotional position into your leadership style will greatly enhance your credibility and effectiveness as a coach. Is it okay to use the first two emotional positions in select situations? If you're passionate, positive, and enthusiastic, then act the way that you feel and encourage others to do the same. The third emotional position, however, should be your guide when there is a clear and present danger of anger, frustration, or cynicism destroying what is good in a team member, the entire department, and the overall work environment.

Applying the Principles of Self-Motivation to Personal Growth and Development

"Motivation" is one of the most misunderstood words in the English language. But it is essential that leaders assimilate the emotionally intelligent aspects of motivation in order to become leaders who effectively coach others.

To become a successful and respected leader, you must first and foremost have a passion for the work of your organization. In our company, not only do we have a passion for the products that we represent, we are also passionate about caring for one another and the people whom we serve.

It should be obvious that self-motivated leaders are always looking for ways to improve performance, productivity, processes, and profit. One natural by-product of a leader's passion is that team members become excited about growing in their vocations to serve as well.

People often ask, "Isn't coaching just about motivating others?" Not exactly. Coaching is a comprehensive, multi-faceted approach to the personal and professional development of one's team members.

Motivation is merely one of the tools in the coaching process. If a leader is going to properly employ motivation as a part of this process, it's important that he or she understand what best-selling author Denis Waitley referred to as the "Four Laws of Motivation":

Law #1: You can't motivate anyone.

As we mentioned earlier, human beings have the three gifts of intellect, emotions, and will. Because of these three tremendous resources, most people willingly exercise their capacity to make hundreds of choices every day about what to think, feel, and do — all without the benefit of a motivational coach.

Anyone who has ever attended a multi-level marketing convention has probably listened to an energetic keynote speaker who riles up an audience of screaming, enthusiastic disciples by telling them that they're all destined to become millionaires. Although the participants leave the meeting with excitement and conviction, research shows us that less than one percent actually attains millionaire status. Why is this? Well, even the best motivational speaker can't motivate anyone, and this is because of the second law of motivation ...

Law #2: All people are motivated.

Suppose two associates in our company have the opportunity to take a class that will help them to advance in their departments, but only one of them signs up for the class. What do we conclude? It's simple. Given a similar set of circumstances behind choosing whether or not to take the class, one associate was motivated to advance while the other was motivated to make a different choice for different reasons. Motivation was a factor in both instances.

Law #3: People do things for their reasons, not yours.

As much as we would like to think that we're ultimately responsible for the choices that our team members make, we are not. If a manager in our company suggests three good reasons why an associate should do something, that individual may have three of their own reasons for not doing it.

One of the keys to successful coaching is to discern the wants, needs, strengths, and challenges of our people and then to collaboratively develop their personal growth and development plan alongside them. When associates take ownership of their personal growth and development, motivation becomes an energizing force that can benefit the individual, the team, and the department.

Law #4: What we identify as a person's weakness is very often just an overextended strength.

Because the fourth law of motivation is commonly considered to be the hardest to master, here's a work-related example of how it applies to good coaching. A company president, Steven, called the performance improvement consultant whom he had engaged to help his organization. He was upset with his relatively new administrative assistant, Brenda. "She's too slow making decisions when I'm not around," he said. "She's been here six months, and the smart, intelligent person I thought I hired is forever mired in a state of analysis paralysis. She still needs me to make a decision on even the most minor issues. I'm thinking of terminating her employment on Monday, but I thought I would ask you if there was any hope to rehabilitate her."

The consultant came to the office and met with Brenda for about an hour. During the meeting, it was obvious that she was a bright, gifted, and talented individual. So why wouldn't she make decisions when the boss wasn't around? It became evident that in her former position with a different company, Brenda was never permitted to make a decision when her supervisor was away—a restriction that actually caused her to seek new employment.

Steven, the company president, had determined that Brenda was someone who wasn't capable of making a decision when she simply hadn't reconciled the over-controlling environment of her recent past with Steven's need for decisions to be made in his absence.

In a short time, Steven realized that Brenda's overextended strength was that she followed directions to the letter. She simply had not put into perspective the directives of her former boss that she never make a decision in his absence.

Over the next several months, the situation improved and Steven was able to successfully work through the obstacles that he had with Brenda. Steven's initial frustration was a microcosm of one of the most intense challenges that any leader faces as they coach their team members—not dwelling on their perceived weaknesses, but identifying and reinforcing their obvious strengths and talents.

Recognizing and Understanding Emotions in Others

The fundamental component of emotional intelligence is empathy. But let's not kid ourselves. When was the last time you heard of anyone being recognized for demonstrating empathy?

While empathy seems to be out of place in commercial enterprises where profit is king, at the Dimmitt Automotive Group empathy is a quality that matters to each and every associate. As our managers try to create a work environment within which people can learn and develop, it is incumbent upon them to see the responsibilities and everyday activities of their team members from the team members' points of view before offering any specific guidance and direction. The timeworn challenge to "walk a mile in my shoes" is sage advice for managers who want to be valued as credible coaches.

One of our veteran service associates who not long ago retired to be with his family shared this story before he left.

When I came to work here I struggled a bit in the beginning. I was trying to figure out how the book knowledge I learned in technician school applied in the actual world of a car dealership. The shop foreman at that time sensed my frustration and took me out for a sandwich one day. He'd been around a long time and shared with me some of the stories of the mistakes and successes he had when he started in the business, including the time he was pouring water into a car where the oil needed to go. For the next couple of months, he'd go out of his way to stop by my stall and ask if there was anything he could do to help me. I never forgot how much his help meant to me as the years passed. It's one of the main reasons that I stayed here so long and it's definitely a message that I'll be sharing with my kids and grandkids.

While empathy may not be a business buzzword, its power as a vehicle for reaching out and positively impacting the lives of others is seriously underestimated.

Managing Relationships Effectively

The final component of emotional intelligence is being able to effectively manage relationships.

It would be naïve to suggest that managing relationships effectively simply means being friendly. Nor does it imply that people walk through the halls of our dealerships slapping their fellow associates on the back and telling them what a great job they're doing.

Managing relationships effectively is the most visible result of emotional intelligence. If your capacity for emotional intelligence is well developed, you'll be able to build and maintain adult-to-adult working relationships. Your communications with others will never resort to parental directives or childish outbursts. And you'll seldom, if ever, be trapped in the vicious triangle of persecutor-rescuer-victim transactions.

Maybe you're not buying any of this emotional intelligence stuff just yet. That's not unusual. Inevitably a cynic will ask, "It seems to me that all of this coaching stuff won't help balance my budget. And as far as emotional intelligence is concerned, what the heck does that have to do with bottom-line profits?"

It's always amusing when people reveal their skepticism about coaching and emotional intelligence. All you need to do is get on Google and search for the phrase "the benefits of emotional intelligence in the workplace" and you'll be reading for quite some time.

Not to bore anyone with numbers, as new studies about emotional intelligence are being released regularly, but a Towers Watson assessment of U.S. and Canadian firms disclosed that companies who do a better job of communicating with their employees financially outperform those who do not. On average, a company with an exceptional communications program delivers a 47% greater return to shareholders than its least communicative competitor.

At the Dimmitt Automotive Group, we're not buying into any corporate skepticism that emotional intelligence and coaching aren't high impact tools when it comes to organizational effectiveness, productivity, and profit. As a matter of fact, in the next chapter we're going to demonstrate a simple yet effective coaching process that works for our people.

Emotional Intelligence & Coaching

Downtown Clearwater in the 1930's.

Work began on The Mansion in 1984 and the dealership moved in during 1986. The building was patterned after a library in Georgia, after Mr. Richard Dimmitt (current and third generation owner) and Doreen Dimmitt traveled the south in search of the ideal design to capture the essence of southern hospitality. Mrs. Dimmitt, whose favorite color is green, created the interior design.

A Coaching Process That Works

USA Today reported that, "businesses are struggling to keep pace with a new generation of young people entering the workforce who have starkly different attitudes and desires than employees over the past few decades."

Among the numerous research studies that have been done about how to engage Gen X and Millennial associates in the workplace, these are two of the more fundamental conclusions: the Gen X crowd wants the opportunity to collaborate with others across the organization, while the Millennial generation wants informal communication and a coaching-style approach from its managers.

Having understood that, and because the labor of coaching implies a process of relationship building for any generation, it is imperative that organizational leaders learn and embrace a simple yet powerfully effective four-phase system that we refer to as "The Coaching Relationship Cycle." As we examine the coaching cycle, keep in mind that there is no beginning or end to this cycle and that all four phases must be present on an ongoing basis whenever coaching occurs in the workplace.

The Affirmation Phase

Affirmation comes first in the coaching cycle. The word "affirmation," as applied in the coaching context, signifies that you as a leader affirm the character, competence, and commitment of every team member whom you're coaching.

Looking for a way to start the affirmation phase on the wrong foot? Walk up to one of your team members and say something like, "Hey Lenny! Your repair orders here aren't written up very efficiently." Comments like that guarantee a failing grade in Coaching 101. That's about as far away from being affirming as you can imagine.

Even if Lenny's ability to write repair orders is in need of improvement, affirmation is the best way to enact meaningful changes to his work product over time. How about this approach instead?

Lenny, I really appreciate the way you handle your responsibilities and the manner in which you relate to our guests. If you have a few minutes tomorrow, I'd like to spend some time talking with you about your repair order write-up process. I have a couple of ideas that I believe would make things smoother and more profitable for you as well as our department. Would the morning or afternoon work best for you?

If Lenny's manager is genuinely interested in helping him to enrich his career, then affirming Lenny's diligence and praising the manner in which he interacts with his customers is a good first step, followed by an offer to assist with skill enhancement. Merely telling him that he's inefficient with his write-ups does nothing but create anger, resentment, and frustration—and it contributes absolutely nothing to boosting his self-esteem.

The Information Phase

Once leaders have a firm grip on the affirmation phase of the coaching relationship cycle, they can proceed to the information phase. The information phase consists of adult-to-adult dialogue between the leader and each team member. The primary skill that a leader needs during the information phase is the ability to effectively communicate. If the flow of meaningful communication is absent in this phase, an inevitable disconnect occurs between the leader and his or her associate.

No one does a worse job for having too much information. The information phase can contain numerous teachable moments while at the same time giving the associate an opportunity to ask questions about the information that he or she is receiving.

During this phase, it really doesn't matter what specific information you need to share with your team members; the essential factor is *how* you share that information. Because communication is the most critical component of this phase, it's important to be aware of and to use effective communication tools so that formal coaching sessions and informal one-to-one interactions are both worthwhile and productive.

Here are some suggestions to ensure that the information phase in your coaching relationships accomplishes its desired results:

- Never assume that the team member whom you are coaching has actually understood what you've had to say. Ask point-blank if you've communicated everything clearly.
- Be honest, direct, and compassionate when you communicate with your team members. In the workplace, where time and integrity are at a premium, there is no room for disingenuous communication.
- Be assertive but not aggressive. Assertiveness leaves no doubt about what you're saying in the mind of the listener; conversely, aggression almost always results in defensiveness.
- Create a work atmosphere that invites communication. Make it a point to actively seek the facts, opinions, and ideas of others.
- Be non-judgmental in your communications.
- People communicate on the four basic levels of facts, feelings, values, and opinions. Understanding the sometime subtle differences among these four levels promotes healthy dialogue.

- Avoid win-lose and "I'm right, you're wrong" communication scenarios. Being able and willing to compromise ensures healthy communication between you and your associates.
- Demonstrate respect for yourself and your team members at all times. By dignifying the worth of every team member, you will create an environment within which mutual trust and respect become the cornerstones of effective communication.
- Own your own messages and be responsible for your own feelings. Using "I" statements rather than "he," "she," "you," or "it" statements is much more effective when personal responsibility and credibility are at stake.
- Seek first to understand, then to be understood. A little empathy goes a long way toward ensuring that your communication with your team members is both meaningful and productive.

The Feedback Phase

While the information phase is founded upon effective communication, the leader who masters the feedback phase of the coaching relationship cycle is one who employs legendary listening skills. The feedback phase is essential because it gives each of your team members the chance to ask questions, clarify a plan of action, or state opinions about a particular issue.

People seldom quit their jobs; more often, they quit their bosses. It's never a good thing when a departing employee says, "I'm leaving this organization because my supervisor never listened to me."

This problem is endemic. At a nationally recognized university, two courses were offered — one in communication and the other in listening. So many people registered for the communication course that the university had to add extra sections. The listening class, however, was canceled because not enough people registered to take it. Everyone wanted to learn how to talk, but no one wanted to learn how to listen.

If you're like most leaders, you've received little or no training on how to listen effectively. You have probably been conditioned to simply disseminate information while focusing upon goals and objectives. Furthermore, the sheer volume of work that you face on a daily basis can pressure you to depersonalize your work environment in favor of time and expedience. Big mistake!

Creating a forum in which your team members can provide feedback is critical to the strength of the coaching relationship that you developed with each of them. Here are some ways you can fortify your listening skills:

- ➤ Listen to your team members openly and attentively. When you try to see things from their perspective, you will foster a welcome climate of cooperation and collaboration.
- ➤ When communication requires follow-up, make sure that you and your colleague establish timely, clear, and specific follow-up actions.
- ➤ When you are speaking with one of your team members, reflect back to that person what you think you heard. It's the best way to avoid any pitfalls in listening.
- ➤ If a team member's communication with you is very detailed, take notes or do whatever else is necessary to receive the information accurately.

- Don't let distractions like phone calls, text messages, and emails interrupt your communication with your team members.
- Not everyone may communicate as well as you do. Always listen with patience and understanding.
- Look for non-verbal cues while you're listening. People's body language can tell you an awful lot about what they're trying to say.
- Don't shoot the messenger. In reacting to what you're hearing, make sure that you separate the content of the message from the person who is delivering it.

The Agreement Phase

If the coaching process stops after the feedback phase, it may produce a few short-term, but very few long-term benefits. The affirmation, information, and feedback phases of the coaching relationship cycle cannot survive alone. They need the agreement phase in order to ensure ongoing personal and professional development among the members of your team.

The purpose of the agreement phase is to bring to fruition what you've affirmed, communicated, and

A Coaching Process That Works

discussed with one of your team members. It's a consensus-seeking phase that results in a decision to act in some capacity. The cornerstone of the agreement phase is a collaborative commitment to action.

In the affirmation phase, we used the example of Lenny and the write-up process. By the time that we conclude the agreement phase, Lenny and his manger should have a specific plan for what's going to change, who is responsible for the actions that will be undertaken, what the expected outcomes of these actions will be, and when a follow-up meeting will be held to track their progress.

The agreement phase is the litmus test of the coaching relationship cycle. If you've done everything spectacularly up until now but fail in the agreement phase, it's a little like hitting a home run and forgetting to step on home plate. It just doesn't count.

When a leader has guided his or her associate through an effective coaching plan, not only does their working relationship become energized and productive, but there is a noticeable improvement in the quality of work performed, costly employee turnover is reduced, guest satisfaction is improved, and teamwork reaches an all time high.

So here's the formula: AFFIRMATION + INFORMATION + FEEDBACK + AGREEMENT = LEGENDARY LEVELS OF PERFORMANCE, PRODUCTIVITY, AND PROFIT.

Making It Fun

People often ask, "Can you have fun at work and still be productive?" My answer seldom varies: "Organizational productivity can be increased in direct proportion to the amount of fun that you're having at work." Thomas Edison summed up the ideal work environment when he asserted, "I never did a day's work in my life. It was all fun."

Most of our customers are either employed or have been employed in the past. They appreciate the joy that is inherent in having fun in the workplace. In similar fashion, they clearly grasp what it means to endure the pain of a thankless job that is devoid of any happiness. Consequently, when they visit our dealerships, it's not hard for them to figure out whether or not we know how to have fun at work.

It is up to the leaders of an organization to establish a healthy foundation for having fun on the job. No one feels much like smiling or enjoying one another's company when the boss is a grouch.

The Great Place to Work Institute is the definitive authority for what a great workplace means. They analyze data from ten million employees in forty-five countries who represent over five thousand organizations of varying sizes and within various industries.

Robert Levering, co-founder of the Institute says, "A great place to work is one in which you trust the people you work for, have pride in what you do, and enjoy the people you work with." The Institute further claims that it would be rare to be named to *Fortune*'s list of the "100 Best Companies to Work For" and not score well on the fun-at-work question.

Fun at work shouldn't be an oxymoron, especially in the automotive business. When people buy a vehicle from our company, it's a naturally exciting time for them. As a way of celebrating that joy, their delivery experience should mirror the happiness and enthusiasm that characterizes the everyday work environment.

It would be presumptuous for me to suggest a series of things that you can do to have fun at work. Every company is different, and what might be extremely enjoyable in one business could be a colossal failure in another. Besides, having fun at work does not begin with recognizing someone's birthday, anniversary of employment, or individual sales achievements.

Fun at work has a more cerebral foundation. In his *New York Times* best-selling book, *The Three Signs of a Miserable Job*, Patrick Lencioni talks about job misery and its three signs: irrelevance, anonymity, and immeasurement.

Employees who feel that their jobs don't matter, who feel that they are nameless faces without unique qualities, and who have no tangible means for assessing their growth and progress on the job will never be in a position to have fun when they come to work.

For this reason, the first task of leadership in any organization is not to schedule a pizza party every Friday for lunch so that rank-and-file employees can have some fun. The critically important work in creating a fun environment is to make certain that they know more about their employees than just their first names. In addition, leaders must be certain that their team members have a clear understanding about how important their jobs are to the overall mission of the organization. And lastly, leaders need to provide their people with a measurement system that allows each team member to observe both personal and team progress.

Dale Carnegie put it succinctly when he said, "People seldom succeed unless they have fun in what they are doing." Success for us as a company involves accomplishing our mission, and we expect to have fun doing it.

Sustainable Competitive Advantage: The Formula

*A*s you read the title of this chapter, it might have appeared that we have all of the answers for achieving a sustainable competitive advantage in the automobile business. Nothing could be further from the truth. We're like any other business—a work in progress.

Having said that, what we've learned on our journey so far is that by understanding, embracing, and implementing those behaviors that constitute a fundamental business success formula, we firmly believe that our long-term vision and mission will be accomplished on an ongoing basis.

Here's the formula that we embrace: ALI + GAI + CEI = SCA. Let me identify the formula and then explain it from my perspective. ALI stands for the Apostolic Loyalty Index. In referring to the employees who come to work with us every day, I could easily have used the term Associate Loyalty Index to indicate that we want to recruit, select, hire, and train associates that are loyal to our company. However, that wouldn't be an adequate explanation of what we mean by ALI.

The word "apostolic" implies a fervent advocacy for a belief or system rather than simply a passive loyalty to a company that an employee only affirms when asked. To the extent that our people feel that we care enough to coach them and to engage them in our culture and business strategy, we then develop that "apostle" who goes on to tell his or her family, friends, and community about how proud and excited they are to help us to accomplish our business plan.

That apostolic loyalty then drives what we refer to as GAI, or the Guest Amazement Index. When a guest visits a business, one of three things happens from a results standpoint. Their expectations are not met, their expectations are met, or there is some value-added outcome that they had not anticipated upon their arrival. In terms of the business processes that they encounter

Sustainable Competitive Advantage: The Formula

during their visit, one of three things will also occur. They will either be dissatisfied, satisfied, or amazed.

When a guest visits and leaves with a value-added outcome and while being pleasantly amazed in some form or fashion, not only is their future loyalty to that business solidified, but they, like the associates at that business, become energized with apostolic fervor and can't wait to tell everyone about what just happened.

Finally, CEI stands for Community Engagement Index. When we started our company nearly one hundred years ago, the heartfelt mission of our family was to become a valued business partner in the community and to serve the needs of our neighbors who came to us seeking our help in providing for their transportation requirements.

It almost sounds too simple to say that people aren't all that different today than they were in 1924 when we began our mission. Sure, the pace of life has been drastically altered, and technology has dramatically reconfigured the landscape of the business world. But don't be fooled. People can still distinguish between a profiteer and a person with a servant's heart.

I'm a firm believer that, to the extent to which we support our families, neighborhoods, charities, and communities for the right reasons, what comes back to us is a level of trust, respect, and engagement that we never expected.

Neither my father nor my grandfather taught me that success was easy. The lessons that I learned from them are the same ones that I want to pass along to my sons. Cultivating an apostolic loyalty with those associates who entrust us with their vocations, while at the same time amazing our guests and engaging our community, will achieve for us — as it will for any other business — a sustainable competitive advantage (SCA) that will permit us to continue to improve everyone's quality of life through service, excellence, and innovation.

The Three Gifts of a Servant's Heart

If you ask the average person to describe the meaning of servant leadership, you will probably hear something like, "Servant leaders are supposed to help their people when they need help." And that's true. But servant leadership involves so much more. Servant leadership begins with an awareness that, within a person's heart, there are three powerful gifts that are capable of transforming a company. These are faith, hope, and love.

Faith

The late Steve Jobs said it succinctly: "It's not faith in technology. It's faith in people." Not only do we have to put faith in our people first, we also need to create an environment where they can increase the faith they have in both themselves and us. The heart of a servant leader is built upon faith.

Rachel was a young woman who came to an airline parts manufacturing company with a high school diploma and no work experience. She was a single mom who was the sole support for her beautiful two-year old daughter.

Rebecca, her supervisor on the altimeter production line, was a seasoned professional who took Rachel under her wing. Sensing her personal and professional insecurity, Rebecca went the extra mile to coach Rachel on the skills that she was lacking and encouraged her veteran team members to look out for Rachel's best interests as well.

There were days when it would have been easier to give up on Rachel and just let her go. She was having trouble balancing her home and work life, and she seemed ready to just give in to her fears and insecurities. But Rebecca wouldn't let that happen.

Fast-forward three years to the annual employee awards ceremony where Rachel receives the company's Persevere & Persist Award for improving her productivity and performance on that line. Normally, this is just a come up to the front of the room, accept your award and the applause, and then return to your place event. Not today.

When Rachel is handed the award, she asks for permission to speak. The company's divisional president hands her the microphone and steps to the side. Rachel clears her throat, raises her eyes from the award to her co-workers, and says, "I know that I was supposed to just go back and sit down but there's something I want to say. About three months after I started working here, I was going to quit. I didn't really believe that I had what it takes to do such precision work. But many of you, especially Rebecca, wouldn't let that happen. You believed in me when I didn't want to believe in myself. And so, for my daughter Kaylee and me, I just want to say thank you from the bottom of my heart."

You can imagine what that twenty-second thank you did for Rebecca and her entire team. More than anything, it demonstrated the power of faith. When servant leaders believe in their people, the fruits of their labor yield a rich harvest.

Hope

The second gift of a servant's heart is hope. The poet Maya Angelou wrote, "God puts rainbows in the clouds so that each of us — in the dreariest and most dreaded moments — can see a possibility of hope."

What all generations of workers need to understand is that hope is more than a wish, a fantasy, or a dream. Hope is born of the desire to not only embrace a vision of the future, but to actively invest the energy that it takes to make that vision a reality.

Anyone can say, "I hope that I win the lottery," or "I hope that my favorite team makes it to the World Series," yet there's absolutely nothing that any of us can do to make that happen. That's not the hope of a servant's heart.

Harold was a line technician at a large utility company. It took less than six months of work for him to earn the nickname Hopeless Harold. Despite the fact that he held his own from a performance standpoint, he was a train riding the tracks to disaster, just waiting for some unexpected adversity to derail him.

Picking up on Harold's cynicism and negativity, Harold's supervisor, Chuck, initiated regular coaching sessions. As it turned out, Harold had moved to the south after working ten years for a similar company in the northeast. While he was always commended for his work there, he was routinely passed over for advancements and promotions. Now, at the age of 37, it seemed clear to him that he was stuck in an inescapable rut, even at his new company.

What Chuck was able to do was outline a training and leadership plan that created for Harold the hope that he needed to see a long-term future in his current setting. With coaching and a concrete plan, hope came to life.

The Trappist monk Thomas Merton said, "Do not depend on the hope of results. You may have to face the fact that your work will be apparently worthless and even achieve no result at all, if not perhaps results opposite to what you expect. As you get used to this idea, you start more and more to concentrate not on the results, but on the value, the rightness, and the truth of the work itself. You gradually struggle less and less for an idea and more and more for specific people. In the end, it is the reality of a personal relationship that saves everything."

As Harold concentrated less and less on struggling for a promotion in his new job, the reality of the personal relationships that he developed with his servant leader Chuck, as well as his teammates, energized him with hope and enriched his vocation.

Love

"Oh, c'mon. Does any servant leader really love their employees?" That's a typical question whenever the words "love" and "workplace" are used in the same sentence.

The role of a servant leader is first and foremost to help team members to develop, grow, and become the people whom they are capable of becoming, both personally and professionally. Embracing that role is one of the supreme acts of love that one person could have for another.

But those are just words. In a more practical vein, here are a few non-negotiable requirements that servant leaders must complete in order to make sure that their team members love them as well.

➢ Be a human being, not an angry boss. If you're always yelling at people, berating them, or embarrassing them in meetings, you've failed the most basic test. No one can love you when you're being disrespectful.

- Do what you say you're going to do when you say you're going to do it. Keeping your word enhances your credibility and creates a sense of security and stability within the work environment.
- Communicate frequently and give honest feedback. Looking people straight in the eye and telling them what's on your mind fosters a great platform for open and constructive dialogue.
- Create a safe environment and ask for honest feedback. It's not just good enough to give feedback, but you have to receive it as well, and then not be defensive or upset when you hear things that you might not want to hear. In addition, maintaining confidentiality is essential for nurturing respect and trust.
- Find out what your people need in order to do a better job and then get it for them. Whether it's equipment, policies, or procedures, enabling people to be successful in their jobs is a sure sign that you care about them.

> Get rid of any drama. Have you heard the expression, "Don't make a mountain out of a molehill?" Do not let minor disagreements, conflicts, and gossip become a soap opera of dysfunction in your business.

> Be compassionate. Individuals leave their families to come to work. And sometimes they leave sick spouses, dying parents, financial turmoil, or other issues that may cause them to be discouraged on any given day. Your sense of compassion during these difficult times will be forever appreciated.

> Recalling Mother Teresa once again, she said, "Not all of us can do great things. But we can do small things with great love." When servant leaders reach out daily in small ways to their team members, this is not only a demonstration of love for their fellow human beings; it can also give life and strength to the very character of a company.

What Does The Future Hold?

When it comes to predicting the future, I'm certain that the automotive business is not unlike any other business. It's both frightening and exciting to think about what's in store for my sons, Richard and Peter, in the decades ahead.

Not only is technology changing the ways in which we do business, but people's wants, needs, and desires are creating a new landscape for the ways that transactions are managed and relationships are developed. For a dealer principal like myself, or for any executive for that matter, to turn a blind eye toward the political and economic arena would be shortsighted and foolish.

The American academic John M. Richardson once said, "When it comes to the future, there are three kinds of people: those who let it happen, those who make it happen, and those who wonder what happened."

Of course, the first step in "making it happen" is to understand the current business climate. It's imperative that we use our creative imaginations to paint a portrait and then define a path for how we will continue to serve the needs of our associates, our guests, and our communities.

Placing a man on the moon was a dream that people thought was impossible, but the technological frontiers in the news today are even more mind-boggling. Dr. Peter H. Diamandis, Chairman and CEO of the non-profit X Prize Foundation, is excited about the fact that we will have 3D printers, similar to the replicator on *Star Trek*, in our offices and homes that can manufacture anything we want. He's also pretty thrilled about lab-on-a-chip technology that will be able to diagnose our ailments on the spot, thereby revolutionizing medicine. Diamandis goes on to say that, with 3D printing, artificial intelligence, and robotics, he expects to see the creation of $100 billion companies in the not too distant future.

All of this excitement begs the question, "What's on the horizon for the automotive industry?" Of course,

What Does The Future Hold?

there's no doubt that technology will continue to shape our future, and we're already responding to that challenge as we learn more about how the marketplace wishes to be engaged.

But as technology defines much of what we do in sales, marketing, and advertising, there's one inevitable reality that should shape the behavior of every automobile dealer who wants to have ongoing success in our business. That reality is that people will continue to buy cars, people will continue to drive cars (even if it's telepathically), and people will continue to need their cars serviced.

Since the beginning of our industry, the automotive environment has been a people business, and it will continue to be a people business in the future. Given that fact, those dealerships that see the wisdom in nurturing and developing servant's hearts in their team members are the ones that will maintain a competitive edge in the market.

Writing about the future, the renowned and respected football coach Tony Dungy said, "The first step toward creating an improved future is developing the ability to envision it. VISION will ignite the fire of passion that fuels our commitment to do WHATEVER IT TAKES to achieve excellence. Only VISION allows us to transform dreams of greatness into the reality of achievement through human action. VISION has no boundaries and knows no limits. Our VISION is what we become in life."

Our vision at the Dimmitt Automotive Group is to continue to grow and to develop as a company that puts people first. With servant's hearts, our deepest desire is to leave a legacy of faith for the associates in whom we believe, a legacy of hope for the guests who continue to put their trust in us, and a legacy of love for the community that has supported us for nearly one hundred years.

My Personal Invitation

Dear Friends,

On behalf of our entire family, I want to extend a heartfelt invitation to each and every one of you to visit our dealerships in the Tampa Bay area. You don't have to be in the market for an automobile to experience our hospitality and meet our friendly associates.

In addition, if you would like more information about The Dimmitt Center for Learning, please contact us at 727-797-7070.

We hope that you'll stay engaged with our mission by frequently visiting our websites at www.dimmitt.com and www.dimmittcares.com.

With a servant's heart,
Richard R. Dimmitt

The Mansion as it stands today.

BIOGRAPHIES

Richard R. Dimmitt

Richard R. Dimmitt is the C.E.O. of the Dimmitt Automotive Group. As a third generation Dimmitt family automobile dealer, he has owned and operated successful automobile dealerships for over thirty years. Mr. Dimmitt has won numerous Master Dealer Awards in addition to being recognized in the community for his countless charitable endeavors. Being a member of one of the few original Clearwater families, Richard prides himself in being able to support and enrich the residents of the Tampa Bay area.

Tom McQueen

Tom McQueen is an award-winning author, nationally-acclaimed speaker and leadership coach.